# Simple Strategies for
## Scrap Quilts

LYNN RODDY BROWN

# Simple Strategies for

# Scrap Quilts

*Martingale*®
& COMPANY

Simple Strategies for Scrap Quilts
© 2006 by Lynn Roddy Brown

That Patchwork Place® is an imprint of
Martingale & Company®.

Martingale & Company
20205 144th Avenue NE
Woodinville, WA 98072-8478 USA
www.martingale-pub.com

Printed in China
11 10 09 08 07 06    8 7 6 5 4 3 2 1

**Library of Congress Cataloging-in-Publication Data**
Library of Congress Control Number: 2006020289

ISBN-13: 978-1-56477-685-3
ISBN-10: 1-56477-685-9

## Credits

President ✦ *Nancy J. Martin*

CEO ✦ *Daniel J. Martin*

COO ✦ *Tom Wierzbicki*

Publisher ✦ *Jane Hamada*

Editorial Director ✦ *Mary V. Green*

Managing Editor ✦ *Tina Cook*

Technical Editor ✦ *Ellen Pahl*

Copy Editor ✦ *Liz McGehee*

Design Director ✦ *Stan Green*

Illustrator ✦ *Robin Strobel*

Cover Designer ✦ *Stan Green*

Text Designer ✦ *Trina Craig*

Photographer ✦ *Brent Kane*

## Mission Statement

Dedicated to providing quality products and service to inspire creativity.

## Dedication

To all the families who, in a time of great sorrow, make the unselfish decision to save lives through organ donation.

## Acknowledgments

I want to thank my husband, Bill, for being my partner on and off the dance floor for more than 40 years. Marrying you was the best decision I ever made.

I also want to thank my children—Kim, Wes, and Nancy—for all you've taught me. My life wouldn't be the same without you.

Thank you to the Blockbuilders of the Quilt Guild of Greater Houston and the Piecemakers of Bellaire United Methodist Church for putting up with my need to lecture and for providing love and support during difficult times. I could not ask for better friends.

Thanks also go to Ruth Barnett, my childhood art teacher, for introducing me to value and color.

The following quilters have written wonderful books and taught inspiring classes. Thank you for teaching me, Sharyn Craig, Harriet Hargrave, Roberta Horton, Alice Kish, Marsha McCloskey, Sally Schneider, and Darra Duffy Williamson.

And thank you, Pat Speth, who told the Quilt Guild of Greater Houston that she just decided to write a quilt book and did it. You made me think maybe I could, too.

# Contents

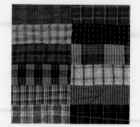

## Texas Two-Step

## Bow Ties

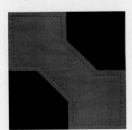

## Spools

## Hourglass

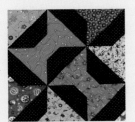

# Introduction

If you've ever wanted to make a scrap quilt and didn't know where to start, or if you've made a scrap quilt that you were less than delighted with, I'm hoping you'll find this book useful.

I've spent the last 13 years making scrap quilts. I've taken classes from the best teachers, read many books, and belonged to a bee that traded blocks. The most important thing that I did was to actually make scrap quilts. Not just one or two, but many. Each quilt was a learning process. Each quilt presented a different challenge. This book is about what I've learned. I hope to give you suggestions and guidelines. I don't believe in rules. The quilt you make should be yours.

It's much easier to be successful with some types of scrap quilts than others. All the quilts in this book use basic rotary cutting and straight sewing, but it's not usually the piecing that makes some scrap quilts more difficult than others. It's the fabric selection. I've rated the skill levels of each quilt in the book from beginner to intermediate in terms of fabric selection. If you start with the easy quilts and are successful, you'll be ready and eager to move to more challenging projects. In terms of piecing, the quilts also range from beginner to intermediate. Here is the system I used for rating the piecing of each quilt:

- ✦ **Beginner:** All squares and/or rectangles in a straight set
- ✦ **Easy:** Beginner blocks in a diagonal set, or blocks using the folded-corner technique
- ✦ **Intermediate:** Blocks that include triangles pieced along the bias edges

All the quilts in this book are made from *scrap strips*. A scrap strip measures 5½" x 20", which is approximately one-third of a fat quarter. Scrap strips came about when I was asked to teach at a retreat and I wanted my students to trade fabrics. The block I wanted to teach was made of four-patch units and triangles. I didn't want students to have to trade two different fabric sizes—strips for the four patches and squares for the triangles. After working with the block, I realized that if the traded scraps were 5½" x 20", both four patches and triangles could be cut from the same piece of fabric.

The great thing about 5½" x 20" pieces is that, even allowing for shrinkage and bad cuts, three scrap strips can almost always be cut from a fat quarter.

"If you've ever wanted to make a scrap quilt and didn't know where to start . . . I'm hoping you'll find this book useful."

# Understanding Scrap Quilts

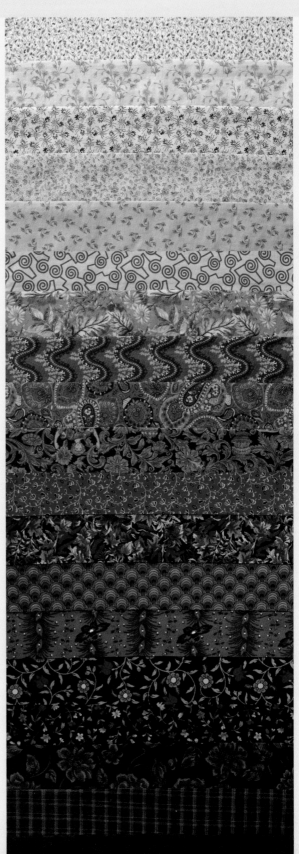

I think the best definition of scrap quilts is in Roberta Horton's book *Scrap Quilts: The Art of Making Do*: "A scrap quilt is impossible to memorize." Scrap quilts look great from a distance and are full of surprises when you get up close. I hate bed making, but when there's a scrap quilt on the bed, I can find joy in all the colors, textures, and patterns as I go through the drudgery. "Orange Blossom Special" (page 46), came off my bed to be in this book.

## Value, Value, Value

In most quilts, it's color that defines the pattern. In scrap quilts, there are many fabrics; therefore, it's value that defines the pattern. So what is value? Value is the relative darkness or lightness of a color. With paint, it's easy to see how values can change. Adding white to red makes pink. The more white, the lighter the pink. If you add black to red, you get burgundy. The more black, the darker the red. With fabric, it's not always easy to determine value. A single fabric print might include several different values.

One way to start a scrap quilt, which I learned in a class taught by Sally Schneider, is to gather all the fabrics you'd like to use. Sort the fabrics into three piles—light, medium, and dark. Don't spend a lot of time sorting. You can always change your mind later. As you look at the piles, you'll probably see the need to create two additional piles—medium-light and medium-dark. Arrange the fabric in order by value as shown.

Look at the fabrics at right. Notice that the fabrics in the medium range have more visual texture. The very light and very dark fabrics have less texture. To be very dark, all the colors in the fabric must be dark. To be very light, all the colors must be light. Visual texture is created when there are several different values. Fabrics with a lot of texture add movement to a quilt.

Look at the examples of the Rail Fence block on this page. The first block uses a very light fabric and a very dark fabric. This gives the block strong, clear lines. The second block also has strong, clear lines, but the middle strip adds texture and is therefore more interesting. The third block uses a light and a medium light for a softer effect. There is still contrast, but it's not as strong as the previous two blocks. The fourth block uses very similar values. The pieced pattern of this block might be lost in a quilt. The fifth block uses a large-scale floral fabric with more than one value. The lines of the block are blurred. None of this is good or bad. You just need to know what you're trying to achieve.

Block 3

Block 1

Block 4

Block 5

Five Rail Fence blocks in different value combinations.

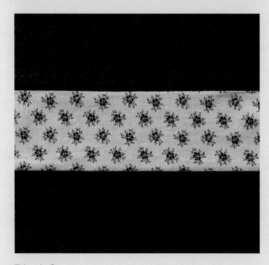

Block 2

Some fabrics are difficult to use. They might not seem to fall into any group, because they contain multiple values. When I was a beginning quilter, I fell in love with the blue-and-white print fabric shown below (top). I bought 15 yards. I was trying to make a Log Cabin block with a dark side and a light side. It took me a long time to understand that this fabric had three values—light, medium, and dark—and therefore couldn't easily be used on either side of the block. Most of this fabric now lives on the back of two large quilts. The fabric on the bottom also contains both light and dark values. When I used this fabric in a block, I ended up with a light spot dead center in what should have been a dark triangle.

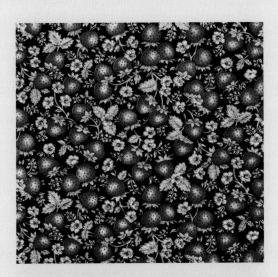

Prints that include strong value contrasts or multiple values might be difficult to categorize by value.

## Types of Scrap Quilts

When I was asked to give a talk on scrap quilts, I was forced to organize my quilts. As I laid them out, they seemed to fall into the groups that I've outlined below. I'm sure other quilters have different ways to organize their quilts, but this is what works for me. The groups are arranged in order of difficulty with what I consider the two easiest groups first.

### A Note about the Quilts

For each quilt in this book, I've indicated the skill level required for both the piecing and the fabric selection. Most projects are easy, especially if you want to duplicate the quilt as shown in the photo. For piecing, only the quilts with triangles have been given a rating more difficult than "easy."

### QUILTS BASED ON COLOR

In this book, quilt designs based on color use two colors each. "Down the Line" (page 60) features blue and yellow. In the blocks, the blues and the yellows are always used in the same positions. Each triangle has a blue side and a yellow side. Each four-patch unit is made with a blue and a yellow.

You could make a color-based quilt with only two fabrics. I've seen some beautiful antique red-and-white quilts. What makes a scrap quilt special are all the different prints and values. If you look closely at the blue-and-yellow quilt, you'll see light yellow to gold and light blue, teal, and dark blue. Some of the fabrics include other colors, but they read as blue or yellow. I've found that even when a quilt is based on color, value also plays an important part. In "Down the Line," most of the blues are darker than the yellows.

Solids

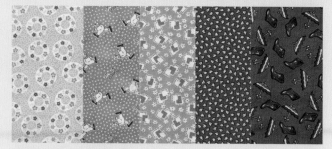

1930s reproductions

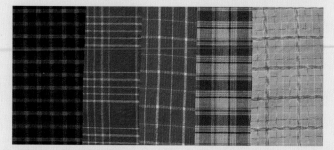

Plaids

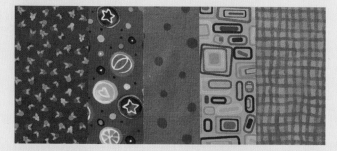

Clear brights

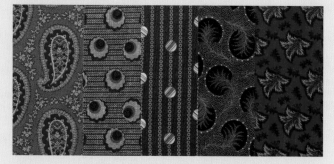

1800s reproductions with other grayed fabrics

## QUILTS WITH GROUPS OF RELATED FABRICS

When I use the term "related fabrics," I don't mean fabrics produced by the same manufacturer designed to be used together. These collections might make a beautiful quilt, but a scrap quilt needs more variety. I used five different groups of related fabrics for the quilts in this book. They're shown at left.

There are many other groups, of course, such as collections of Asian fabrics, florals, and batiks. Several quilts in this book are made entirely from related fabrics. Others use a common fabric either in the background or in the same position in the block. "Glo in the Dark" (page 29) and "Nana's Pinwheels" (page 83) use only related fabrics. "Floating Spools" (page 79) features a dark background while "Nana's Scrap Quilt" (page 42) has a light background. The important thing is that there is contrast between the fabric group and the background. "Love to Mary" (page 32) uses the same light fabric in the center of all the blocks.

## STAND-ALONE BLOCKS

In the quilt "Scrappy Spools" on page 76, two fabrics were chosen for each block—a dark for the spool and a light for the background. Each spool is seen as an individual block. The first block shown below has strong contrast between the spool and the background. This is the formula used for most of the blocks in the quilt. In her book *Sensational Scrap Quilts*, Darra Duffy Williamson says she will "establish the pattern of a quilt" and then alter one out of four blocks. "The occasional shift in values . . . adds to the impact of the quilt."

When making additional blocks, I tried to follow Darra's suggestion. The second block (on the previous page) has contrast but uses a lighter value for the spool. The third uses a darker background. The pattern in these final two blocks might disappear when viewed from a distance. I discovered that the shifts in value often caused oval shapes to form. This occurs when the spools have a similar value to the backgrounds of adjacent blocks as shown below.

"Thank You, Marsha" on page 88 is a quilt based on color but it also has stand-alone blocks. I paired pink with brown, made two Star blocks, and then picked another pink and brown for the next set of blocks. For a scrappier look, the blocks could be made by pairing very different fabrics and altering the backgrounds as shown below.

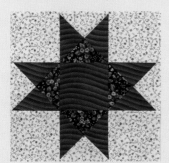

To add interest, the backgrounds of a few blocks could be darker, have unusual visual textures, or use values that would cause the star points to be lost as shown above right.

If you find delight in combining fabrics that look great next to each other, you will enjoy making this type of quilt.

## ALL SCRAPS WITH AN OVERALL PATTERN

"Wild West Shuffle" (page 64) and "Bow Tie Circles" (page 72) are good examples of quilts made entirely from scraps, in which value creates an overall design. To make these quilts, I first sorted all the fabric I planned to use into two groups: (1) medium through dark and (2) light. For an overall pattern to be established, there must be good contrast between the piles. I didn't use medium-light fabrics or ones that mixed values within a print. Some of the fabrics used in these quilts are shown at the bottom of the page.

Notice that there's a gap in value between the darkest light and the lightest medium-dark fabrics. Fabrics that fit into the gap often make good setting triangles or a first inner border, because they contrast with the values used in the blocks. Also notice the wide range of textures in this grouping. If the values are correct, you can use very different fabrics that don't seem to go together. It is the value that ultimately forms the pattern.

Gap in value
↓

# Collecting Fabric

All the quilts in this book are made using the same size *scrap strip*, which measures 5½" x 20". This size is easy to cut and trade. I wanted people who didn't have a large fabric collection of to be able to acquire enough variety to make a successful scrap quilt. Trading is a fun thing to do in a guild or other group of quilters. In the construction of some blocks, there will be leftover fabric. I designed a quilt just for those leftovers: "A Little Bit of Everything" (page 36) is a totally scrappy quilt that uses pieces measuring 2" x 5½".

## Stash

Have you ever asked a quilting friend, "What are you going to do with all that fabric?" If you have, it's obvious that you don't understand the concept of a stash. A stash is all the fabric that a quilter has bought just because she loves it. Owning it is enough. It's also all the fabric that was bought with a project in mind and then a more exciting project came along. Leftover fabric from finished projects also qualifies. Every quilter is entitled to a stash. A stash is to a quilter what paint is to an artist.

The great thing about scrap quilts is that you can use a piece of one of your favorite stash fabrics and not use it up. What's even more exciting is that you can use it in several quilts. When I have a fabric that I know works well, I'll buy more. If it's on the sale table, I buy a lot more. I see nothing wrong with this. When your pantry gets low on green beans, you buy more green beans, right?

If you have a stash, consider cutting a 5½" x 20" piece from some of your fabrics. Start with the ones you wonder why you ever bought and go from there. Usually the really "ugly" fabrics work best in scrap quilts.

I have one thing to say about stashes that I first heard from Mary Ellen Hopkins: if you can't find it, you don't have it. If you're going to effectively use your stash, it must be organized. I use plastic bins. Some of my fabrics are sorted by color. Others or organized by print: plaids, stripes, florals, and my really "ugly" multicolor fabrics, which work so well in scrap quilts. I have bins for specific fabric types, such as 1930s reproduction prints, clear brights, and 1800s reproductions. Any system that works for you is fine—you just need to have one.

## Fat Quarters

Fat quarters are approximately 18" x 21". This is equal to one-fourth of a yard but is a much more useful size for a quilter than a typical quarter-yard cut that is 9" x 42". Fat quarters are like going to a potluck dinner. You get to have lots of variety, just not as much of any one thing. The scrap strips used for all the quilts in this book are 5½" x 20", approximately one-third of a fat quarter. From each fat quarter, you can cut three scrap strips.

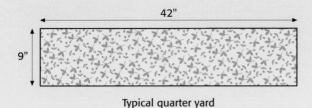

Typical quarter yard

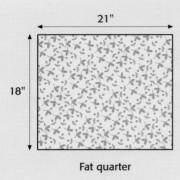

Fat quarter

### Fun Ways to Acquire Scraps

Go shopping with two friends and buy fat quarters. Divide each fat quarter into three scrap strips and swap.

Organize a fabric trade in your guild or quilting group. Make sure that everyone understands that you're trading only good-quality 100%-cotton fabric that has been washed and carefully cut.

Visit quilt shops when you travel, and collect fat quarters from different regions.

## Block Trades

Another way to get lots of variety in scrap quilts is to trade blocks. For nine years I've belonged to a bee that trades blocks. This has forced me to think outside my box, and it's a good learning opportunity. The block that uses the "ugly" fabric I would never have bought, or that features a putrid greenish gold I cannot stand, might be just the thing to give a quilt life. If you trade only fabrics, you will still use only your favorites. If a block is made, you are more likely to give it a chance.

## What to Buy

The sale table is a great place to shop. These are the fabrics that didn't sell well. They often have great texture, unusual patterns, and not-so-pleasing colors. Look for medium to dark fabrics that don't have large areas of very light colors. Select fabrics in which all the colors within a piece are about the same value. Avoid fabrics that have only one color, known to quilters as tone-on-tones. These fabrics may be beautiful, but generally, they don't add much interest and you probably already have lots of these. Most quilters don't have enough light fabrics. These are not very exciting, but you need them. I think of fabrics with white or beige backgrounds as lights, and those with pastel backgrounds as medium lights.

When I'm buying from sale tables, I buy at least a yard. This fabric will go into my stash for future use. A yard is usually enough for setting triangles, sashing, binding, or a narrow border. Of course, it's also enough to make blocks.

# Getting Started: Basic Quiltmaking

In this section I've included many of my favorite techniques and helpful hints. Check out some of the excellent quiltmaking books at your local quilt shop if you're a beginner and need further information about a specific topic.

## Equipment

In addition to standard sewing supplies and rotary-cutting equipment, here are a few specific items that will help you be successful in your quiltmaking.

**Single-hole throat plate.** If you don't have one for your machine, you may be able to buy one from your sewing machine dealer. You'll have fewer problems with balled thread and triangle points being pushed down the hole.

**Rulers.** I believe in lots of rulers. If a special ruler will make a technique easier, I buy it. For the projects in this book, you'll need at least a 6" or 6½" x 24" ruler and an 8" square with a diagonal line. A 15" square is handy for cutting setting triangles and squaring up corners of your quilt. Use only rulers made for rotary cutting.

**Pins.** I use lots of pins and am very particular about which ones I buy. Mine are 1⅜" superfine silk pins with glass heads.

**Seam rippers.** I have several. If I need a seam ripper, I'm already aggravated. I don't need to be further aggravated when I cannot find one.

**Tweezers.** I did without these for years, but I don't know how. I use a sturdy 5" pair of tweezers to grab short threads at the sewing machine. I really love them when I'm machine quilting. They're strong enough to open and remove the safety pins when I run the machine too close.

**Design wall.** My design wall consists of two sheets of stiff insulation board covered with flannel. It's propped against my den wall. In the early years, my husband hauled it to the garage when we entertained. One Thanksgiving, I had about a hundred blocks carefully arranged. The wall didn't go to the garage that day and it has not been there since, but my husband still won't let me nail it in place.

**Thread.** I only use good-quality 50/3 100%-cotton thread. For piecing scrap quilts, I use a light beige or medium gray color. When I machine quilt borders and setting triangles, I match the thread color to the fabric. For the interior of the quilt, I usually use a medium-value neutral color.

**Tape measure.** A 120" tape measure is great for measuring quilts.

## Rotary Cutting

A rotary cutter is a rolling razor blade. They're wonderful, but they're very dangerous and must be used with care. Follow these guidelines and make them a habit.

+ Close your cutter every time you put it down.
+ Replace your blade often and anytime it gets a nick.
+ Be sure that you don't have the blade screwed down too tight. The blade needs to roll easily.
+ Always wash and press your fabric before cutting. Wrinkles and folds will result in inaccuracies in your cutting.

### CUTTING STRIPS

When I have a large piece of fabric—more than a yard—to cut into strips, I tear off approximately a yard before cutting. I find working with a large piece too difficult to keep straight on the cutting mat.

1.  Fold the fabric with the selvages together and lay the fabric on the mat with the fold toward you. Make sure you have a smooth fold. Place your long ruler on the left edge of the fabric so that it covers both layers of the raw edge. Use a square ruler along the fold to align the longer ruler as shown. Remove the square ruler and make the cut so that you'll have a clean, straight edge.

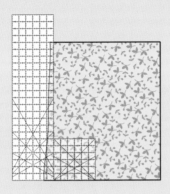

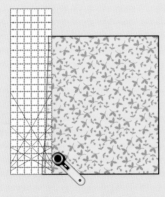

2.  To cut strips, align the newly cut edge with the desired width on the ruler and cut. Restraighten the edge of your fabric after cutting three or four strips.

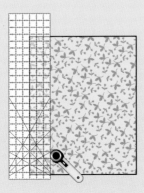

## CUTTING SCRAP STRIPS

All the quilts in this book use scrap strips that measure 5½" by approximately 20".

**To cut scrap strips from a fat quarter,** first wash and press the fabric. Lay the fabric on the cutting mat, with the selvage edge across the top. Fold the bottom raw edge up to meet the selvage. It's more important for the fold to be smooth than for the edges to align. The fold should measure approximately 18". You need a minimum of 16½". Straighten the left edge as in step 1 of "Cutting Strips." Then cut three 5½"-wide strips. There is no need to trim them to exactly 20". If your strips are longer than that, it will give you a little extra insurance later on.

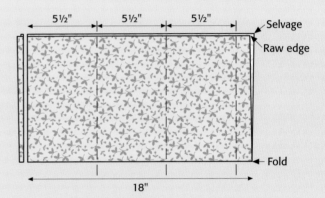

**To cut scrap strips from yardage,** follow the directions for cutting strips. Cut the strips 5½" wide by 40" (or the width of your fabric). Cut each strip in half, creating two 5½" x 20" strips. Six scrap strips can be cut from ½ yard of fabric, and 12 can be cut from 1 yard.

## Machine Piecing

All the quilts in this book are pieced using straight seams and an accurate ¼" seam allowance. All cutting measurements include the seam allowances.

### SEWING AN ACCURATE ¼" SEAM

It's important for seams to be sewn an accurate ¼". I use a seam gauge that screws down to the bed of my machine. Many quilters use a ¼" foot on their sewing machine or a seam guide. To make a seam guide, place a rotary ruler under the presser foot. Position the ruler so that when the needle is lowered, it falls on the ¼" mark. Make certain the ruler is square with the machine. Place a seam gauge, moleskin, painter's tape, or quilter's masking tape next to the edge of the ruler and use that as a guide when sewing.

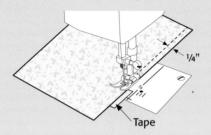

## CHAIN PIECING

Chain piecing is a technique that saves time and thread. To chain piece, place pairs of units right sides together under the presser foot. Sew off the edge of the fabric. Feed the next pair without lifting the presser foot or cutting the thread. Continue until all pairs are sewn, and then clip the threads between pieces.

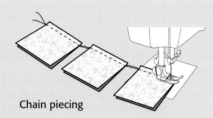

Chain piecing

### Assembly-Line Piecing

Arrange all the units for a block in a logical stitching order to the left of your machine. Organize the units for the other blocks in the same way and stitch nonstop for as long as you can.

I pin all places where seam lines or points meet. I often start with a pin pushed straight through these points. I hold this "positioning pin" perpendicular to the fabric and then place pins on each side.

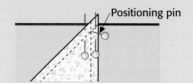 

Positioning pin

Units with seams pressed to one side, in opposite directions, can easily be matched. Make certain the opposing seams are pushed tightly together—butted—then pin.

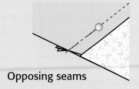 

Opposing seams

## Pressing

After sewing each seam, press it flat as it was sewn to set the seam. Then press the seam open or to one side before sewing the next piece to it. Usually seams are pressed to one side, toward the darker fabric. In the project instructions, I suggest that you press many of the seams open. I do this because I machine quilt all my quilts, and pressing the seams open creates a smoother, flatter surface with less skipping and thread breakage. I use quilting patterns that cross over the seams, thereby stabilizing and holding them together. If you're planning to outline the quilt patches either by hand or machine—or tie the quilt—you might want to press all the seams to the side.

## Constructing Units from Paired Fabrics

When working with scrap strips, I've found an efficient and accurate way to cut and piece units. For most of the quilts in this book, you'll be instructed to pair up your fabrics before cutting. The method is called "paired fabrics."

1.  Using the two fabrics that will be sewn together, lay the first fabric, right side up, on the ironing board. Spray evenly with spray starch.

2.  Lay the second fabric, right side down, on top of the first, aligning the edges, and press well. I like to use a steam iron. The fabrics should now be smooth, crisp, lightly stuck together, and ready to cut.

## FOUR-PATCH UNITS

1.  Pair two fabrics to be sewn together as described above, and then straighten the left edge with a ruler and rotary cutter. Cut the required number of 2½" segments.

2.  Sew each segment along one long edge.

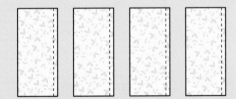

3.  Set the seams and press toward the darker fabric. You've created small strip sets. Pair the strip sets, placing them right sides together and making certain the seams are opposing. Lay each unit on the cutting mat, with the dark end of the strip set at the top. Trim the left edge and then cut two 2½" segments. I like to place one pin in the cross seam to hold the pieces together before I remove the units from the cutting mat.

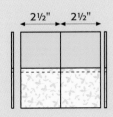

4.  Sew each segment along one long side. Set the seams and press open.

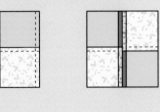

## HALF-SQUARE-TRIANGLE UNITS

1.  Using the two fabrics that will be sewn together, make paired fabrics as described above.

2.  Cut the required number of squares from the two layers. Cut these paired squares on the diagonal. I like to place one pin in the units to hold the pieces together before removing them from the cutting mat.

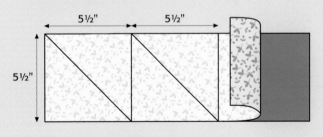

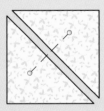

3.  Sew the diagonal seams. Set the seams and press toward the darker fabric.

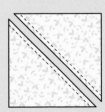
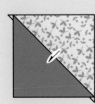

4. I always make half-square-triangle units slightly oversized. Use a small, square ruler with a diagonal line to trim and square up the unit. Position the diagonal line on the seam of the unit with the fabric extending just beyond the edge of the ruler. Trim the two adjacent sides.

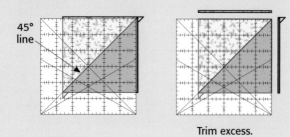

Trim excess.

5. Rotate the unit and position the ruler so that the two trimmed edges of the unit are on the ruler lines for the required size. Trim the excess fabric from the remaining two sides.

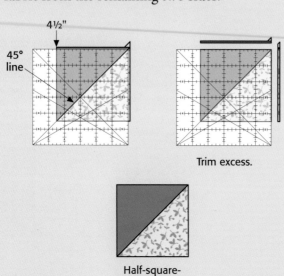

Trim excess.

Half-square-
triangle unit

## Folded-Corner Triangles

1. Using the small squares as instructed in the project directions, fold each one in half on the diagonal with *wrong sides together* and press.

Fold and crease.

2. Following the diagram for your project, place a pressed square on a corner, right sides together. Using the crease as a sewing line, sew one thread width outside the crease.

3. Trim away the excess fabric ¼" from the line of stitching. Set the seam and press outward. Repeat until all folded-corner triangles are complete.

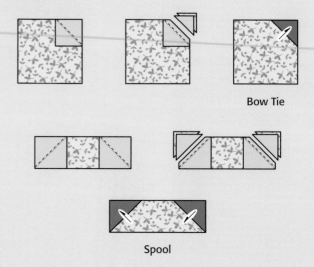

Bow Tie

Spool

# Designing with Scrap Blocks

I think the most important thing about making scrap quilts is to keep an open mind. The second most important thing is to have a design wall. A stack of scrap blocks and a design wall are all you need for hours of fun and endless possibilities for creativity. When I make quilts, I usually start with a plan, but very often during the design process, an entirely different quilt emerges.

Even if you're trying to duplicate a quilt in this book, your quilt will be uniquely yours because your fabrics will be unique. My quilt may have a blue border, but with your fabric collection, red may be a better choice. I never choose or buy a border fabric until I've put the top together. If I can't find border fabric in my stash, I take the top with me when I shop.

## Advantages of Scrap Quilts

You never run out of fabric.

You won't get bored making the same block out of the same fabrics.

You don't have to worry about finding perfectly matching fabrics; if you have nine reds (or any other color), the tenth will blend with the others.

If you decide to make a larger quilt, you just need to acquire more scraps and make additional blocks.

If you're tired of making blocks, you can stop and make a smaller quilt.

Scrap quilts can be made from your stash. Everyone knows that stash quilts are free.

You can buy any fabric you want and know that it can go into a scrap quilt.

When making any quilt, I make about two-thirds of the blocks required. I put them on the design wall and then decide which direction I'd like to go with the remaining third. Doing this gives me more options than if I wait to start the design process after all the blocks are made.

Once I have the blocks on the wall, I turn my back, walk away, turn back to the wall, and pay attention to my first reaction. Roberta Horton says your first reaction is the one you should go with. Maybe I love the purple. I might see a pink that doesn't go with anything else in the quilt. I notice that all the green is in one corner. The quilt is boring. So what now?

## Go with What You Like

If the purple looks good, select and cut several more purple scrap strips. Make sure the purples are different shades and textures from the purple already in the quilt. You might begin thinking about purple for the main border. If you use a purple border, the purple blocks in the quilt will be the first ones you see, and the quilt will become a purple quilt.

## Take It Out, Add More, Build a Bridge

When a block doesn't seem to go with the rest of the quilt, it's often the intensity of the color that's off. Maybe one pink block is clear and bright and the other pinks are grayed. Sometimes it's best to take the single block out. Another solution is to add more pink. This keeps the original pink from being a focal point. Usually, an odd number of a strong color works best. Include three, five, or seven pieces of different pinks scattered over the surface of the quilt.

The last option is to build a bridge, a technique I learned from Jinny Beyer. Maybe there are reds in the quilt. If you add a couple of reds that have a pinkish cast and a few pinks that lean toward red, then the color differences won't be as stark.

## Scatter the Colors and Textures

If all the green is in one corner, move some of the blocks to scatter the color. The quilts in this book use sets of blocks made from the same fabrics. If there are four blocks in the set, I put them in different quarters of the quilt. If there are two blocks, I put one in the top half and one in the bottom. When choosing fabrics for blocks, be sure each set has a variety of colors and textures. If you scatter the blocks, the colors and textures will also be scattered.

## Jazz Up a Boring Quilt

If you feel your quilt is boring or lacks something, read on for several options that will spice it up and add that spark to take it from boring to exciting.

### ADD DIAGONAL LINES

Diagonal lines add interest, causing the viewer's eye to move across the surface of the quilt. If you're just beginning to make your quilt, you might choose blocks that have a built-in diagonal pattern, such as Double Four Patch, Texas Two-Step, and Bow Ties. These blocks offer many design possibilities. Simply arranging the blocks in straight rows results in a strong diagonal in your quilt. See "Down the Line" (page 60) and "Amish Bow Ties" (page 68).

Arranging the blocks in groups of four to create an "x" results in diagonal patterns going in two directions, such as in "Wild West Shuffle" (page 64) and "Bow Tie Circles" (page 72). "Echoing Squares" (page 56) is an example of blocks arranged in a barn-raising set. Any block with a diagonal line can be used in these sets.

If you've already made your blocks, try setting them on point to create diagonal lines. "Love to

"Down the Line" (page 60)

"Bow Tie Circles" (page 72)

Mary" (page 32) and "Floating Spools" (page 79) are examples.

### ADD COLOR

I don't know a lot about color theory, but red, yellow, gold, and teal are strong colors that will stand out from the rest. A little goes a long way. A few blocks using these colors will perk up the most boring quilt. These colors also work well for inner borders, creating a strong line to frame a quilt.

Mary Ellen Hopkins says purple goes with everything. I put purple borders on the first three scrap quilts I made, and it worked. One of these quilts has a teal inner border, and it's still a favorite.

## OTHER TIPS

If you're having trouble with value, try viewing the quilt in dim light. I do this in the evenings, as it's getting dark. Different levels of light show me different things. My design wall is across from a sliding glass door. I'll often study the reflection of the quilt in the glass and see things I wouldn't see otherwise. Taking digital photos and viewing them on the computer can also be a great help in making design decisions.

## Arranging the Blocks: Quilt Sets

A quilt set or setting is how the blocks in a quilt are arranged. The quilts in this book are set in one of three different ways. You can always choose a different set from the one shown in the photograph.

Whenever there are sashing strips, setting triangles, or plain alternate blocks in a quilt setting, I suggest that you wait until all the blocks are sewn before cutting those elements of the quilt. Your blocks may vary from the exact size by ⅛" or more due to slight differences in cutting and piecing. Measure your blocks and then cut those pieces to fit your blocks. Your quilt will go together much easier this way.

## STRAIGHT SETS

In straight sets, blocks are simply sewn together into horizontal rows. The rows are joined to complete the top. When joining the rows, be sure to carefully match the vertical seams of each row with the next. I pin all of these intersections.

## VERTICAL STRIPPY SETS

"A Little Bit of Everything" (page 36) and "Almost All My Plaids" (page 39) are examples of a strippy set. Blocks are sewn together into panels to create vertical rows. Strips of plain fabric separate the pieced panels. Keep in mind that blocks other than bars can be used in this type of set.

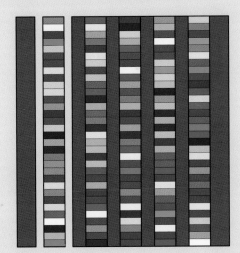

1.  Measure all the pieced panels to make certain that they're the same length. Make adjustments if necessary. Cut the sashing strips the same length as the pieced panels.

2.  Mark the middle and quarter points on the panels and the strips.

3.  Place the panels and strips right sides together, matching ends, quarter points, and the middle. Pin and sew the seams. Press the seams toward the sashing strips.

---

### Tips for Fitting Blocks Together

If you've traded blocks and they're not all quite the same size, here are some tips for making them fit together easier.

+ Use a steam iron to square up and shrink blocks that are too large and to stretch blocks that are too small.

+ Place the larger block on the bottom when joining to a smaller block. The feed dogs will help to ease the extra fabric in.

+ If the size difference is less than ⅛", center the smaller block on the larger block.

+ If the size difference is greater than ¼", don't use the block or remake it. Remember, it's okay to reject a block.

+ Be sure the seams are correctly pressed. The blocks may be too small because of pressed-in tucks.

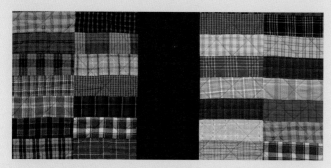

"Almost All My Plaids" detail (See page 39 for full quilt)

## DIAGONAL SETS

In diagonal sets, the blocks are placed on point. This requires side-setting triangles and corner triangles. Throughout the project instructions, the side- and corner-setting triangles are cut larger than necessary. This allows for minor piecing errors and gives you an extra margin of insurance.

1.  Sew the blocks together in diagonal rows, adding the side-setting triangles to the ends. To add the side-setting triangles, first align the corners. Allow the point of the triangle to extend beyond the block as shown. Sew the seam, press toward the triangle, and then trim the point. Sew the diagonal rows together. Add the corner triangles last.

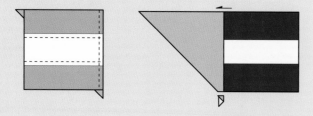

2.  Trim the edges of the quilt top to ¼" before adding borders. Align the ¼" mark of a rotary ruler on the block points as shown.

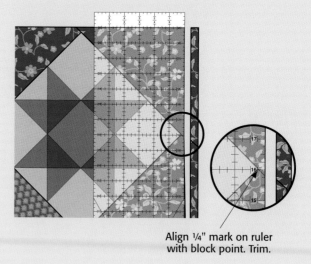

Align ¼" mark on ruler with block point. Trim.

## Tips for Joining Blocks

No matter which set you use, you need to keep the blocks or pieced panels in the correct order when moving them from the design wall to the sewing machine. I write numbers on small pieces of paper about an inch square. If there are 10 blocks in a row, then row 1 will use the numbers 1–10, row 2 will use 11–20, and row 3 will use 21–30. You could use a numbering system that uses letters with numbers. A-1 would be the first block in row A. I consistently pin the numbers to the upper-left corner of each block. I remove one row of blocks and take them to the machine. As I pin the blocks, I make certain the numbers are still in order. When a row is sewn, I carefully press it and return it to the wall. Often, when I return a row to the wall, I'll see things I didn't see before and decide to move or replace a few blocks.

# Finishing the Quilt

Now that you've finalized your design and the blocks are sewn together, you're ready to add borders and complete your quilt. The following sections cover the basic information you'll need, from borders to binding.

## Borders

Most of the quilts in this book have a narrow inner border and a wider outer border. Yardage is given for cutting the outer borders from the lengthwise grain. This requires more fabric but has the advantage of being less stretchy than the crosswise grain. Borders cut on the lengthwise grain help keep the quilt square and flat, and you won't need to piece the border strips. The inner borders are cut from the crosswise grain and are pieced, when necessary, to get the required length.

### JOINING BORDER STRIPS

Border strips may be joined using a straight seam or a diagonal seam. I prefer a diagonal seam because I think it's less noticeable. If I use a stripe for the inner border, I match the stripe and join strips with a straight seam. Press border seams open.

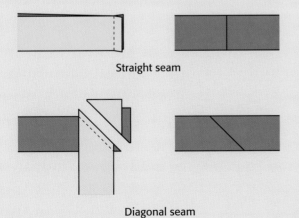

Straight seam

Diagonal seam

### ADDING BORDERS

Always measure the quilt top through the middle to determine the border lengths, as the outer edges are often stretched slightly from handling.

1. Lay the quilt out on a smooth surface. Measure lengthwise through the middle. Use this measurement to cut side borders from the lengthwise grain. Mark the middle and quarter points.

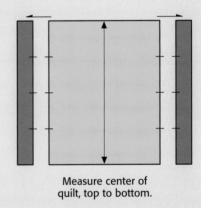

Measure center of quilt, top to bottom.

2. Place the borders on the quilt top, right sides together, matching the ends, quarter points, and middle. Pin carefully. If the top edges have stretched so that they're longer than the borders, take the top with the pinned border attached to the ironing board. With the top facing up, use a steam iron until the top can be eased to fit the border. Add additional pins before removing the top from the ironing board.

3. Stitch the top to the border, with the pieced side facing up. This allows you to see any triangle points that need to be sewn through and helps prevent seams from flipping. A walking foot is a tremendous help when sewing borders. Press toward the border.

4. Measure the width of the quilt top across the middle, including the side borders just added. Cut the borders to this length and sew them to the top and bottom as you did the sides.

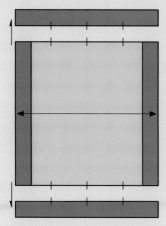

Measure center of quilt, side to side, including border strips.

5. Repeat the steps to add any remaining borders.

## Layering and Basting

Instructions with each project will tell you how to piece the backing. After piecing, trim it to 4" larger than your quilt top on all sides. The batting should also be at least 4" larger all around.

I machine quilt and use 1" safety pins to baste. If you plan to hand quilt, baste with thread in a grid about every 6". Before basting, make sure the backing and top are well pressed. I throw my batting in the clothes dryer on low heat for a few minutes to remove wrinkles.

Secure the backing right side down to a table with masking tape or binder clips. Before pinning,

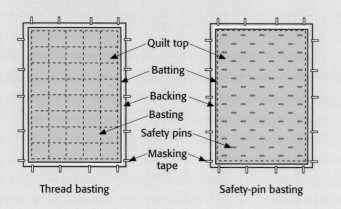

Quilt top
Batting
Backing
Basting
Safety pins
Masking tape

Thread basting            Safety-pin basting

decide where the quilting lines will go. If I plan to cross the middle of a block, I'll pin the edges of the block. Pin along the sides of the inner borders to keep them straight. Place pins about a fist width apart.

## Pin-Basting Details

I baste on a waist-high, drop-leaf sewing table that measures 40" x 72". This table is one of my best investments. Before this, I used an office table that could be folded and stored. Quilt shops often let you borrow their tables if you ask in advance. The table must have a top that will not be damaged by safety pins and a lip narrow enough to use binder clamps.

First I mark the middle of the table and the middle of all four sides. If you use tape or a marker you will not see the lines once you have the backing on the table. I tape a flat button to the middle of the table and toothpicks along the sides at the mid-points. I can feel these "marks" through all three layers—backing, batting, and quilt top.

Place the backing on the table right side down. Feeling for the marks, center it on the table. To clamp the backing to the table, I use 2" binder clamps, purchased at an office supply store. I make sure the back is pulled very tight. This helps eliminate tucks during the quilting. If the quilt is shorter than the table, I use painter's tape to secure the ends.

Using the marks, center the batting over the backing. Carefully center the top over the batting. I make certain the narrow inner borders are straight by aligning them with the edges of the table.

When I have pinned as much of the quilt surface as is on the table, I remove the binder clamps and shift the quilt to one side. Because the middle of the quilt is pinned, I clamp only three sides to the table. Fold back the top and batting. Clamp three sides of the backing to the table. The weight of the quilt will pull the fourth side tight. Smooth the batting and the top back over the reclamped backing. Continue pinning and repositioning the quilt until the entire top is pinned.

## Tips for Machine Quilting

Begin with a carefully pieced and pressed quilt top.

Quilt on a flat surface that supports the quilt. Make sure the quilt can move and slide easily. The instant you feel drag, stop and reposition the quilt.

Topstitch the inner borders with a walking foot a scant ⅛" away from the seam on both sides to anchor and stabilize the quilt. You  may need to use two different thread colors—one to match the inner border and one to match the outer border.

After stabilizing the inner border, quilt the outer border. Hold the extra batting and backing with your right hand while quilting the border.

After the borders are quilted, trim and bind the quilt. Doing this removes all the excess batting and backing and makes the middle of the quilt easier to get under the machine.

## Binding

Bindings can be cut on the bias or on the straight of grain. In my experience, bias bindings wear longer, and the hand sewing seems easier to manage. Stripes or plaids cut on the bias make a lovely binding. Straight-grain bindings, however, use less fabric, stretch less, and are easier to cut. Straight-grain bindings will help hold a wall hanging square.

The cutting instructions for each quilt provide the number of straight-grain strips to cut for binding. If I've used a stripe or plaid cut on the bias, I've included the yardage needed for bias strips and the total number of inches needed as well. I cut my strips 2½" wide for a ⅜" finished binding. For bias strips, cut at a 45° angle across the center of the fabric to get the longest strips possible.

1.  Join the binding strips with diagonal seams, referring to "Joining Border Strips" on page 25. Press the seams open. Fold the binding lengthwise, wrong sides together, and press.

2.  I sew with a seam gauge and trim the quilt before attaching the binding. First stitch around the entire quilt ⅛" from the edge of the quilt top, using a walking foot.

3.  Use a large, square ruler and a long ruler to trim the quilt and make sure that the corners are square. Align the rulers with the inner border or a seam in the patchwork. If a quilt has a plain border, I trim to the edge of the fabric. If your quilt has blocks along the outer edge, such as "Scrappy Spools" (page 76) and "Bow Tie Circles" (page 72), first make sure the corner blocks are square. If they aren't, pin them square and use steam to set them. Since I use a ⅜" seam to attach the binding, I trim ⅛" away from the edge of the blocks.

Stitch ⅛" in from edge of quilt top.
Trim back and batting ⅛" beyond quilt top edge.

4.  To avoid having a binding seam fall at a corner of the quilt, place the binding around the quilt, using a few pins. I start on the top edge and position the binding so that the first binding seam will be sewn before I turn the upper-right corner. I continue placing the binding around the entire quilt, folding it at the quilt corners. If a binding seam hits a corner of the quilt, I reposition the entire binding. When I'm sure the binding is starting in the correct position, I remove all the pins except the one at the starting point.

5.  Begin stitching 6" from the start of the binding, using a ⅜" seam allowance. Bring the bobbin thread up and stitch a few inches. As you approach the first corner, stop the machine and use a small ruler to mark ⅜" from the raw edge of the corner. Sew to the mark and backstitch three stitches.

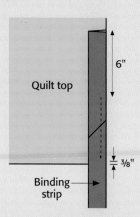

6.  Remove the quilt from the machine. Fold the binding back on itself to create a 45° angle. Turn the binding down to make a fold in the binding that is in line with the upper raw edge of the quilt top. Pin. Be absolutely sure that the fold does not extend beyond the quilt top. Put the quilt back under the presser foot. Lower the needle about ⅛" away from the top fold, pull up the bobbin thread, sew three stitches, backstitch three stitches, and then continue sewing until you approach the next corner. Repeat all the steps for each corner.

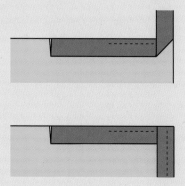

7.  When stitching the last side, stop approximately 12" from the starting point. Remove the quilt from the machine. Fold the unstitched binding edges back on themselves so they just meet in the middle over the unsewn area of the quilt top. Press the folds.

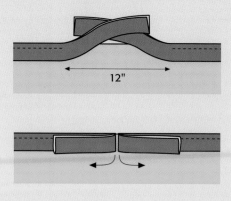

8.  The easiest way to join the binding ends is to trim the ends straight across, ¼" out from the fold lines. Sew the seam. Press it open. Re-press the binding. Make certain the binding fits the unsewn area and finish sewing it to the quilt.

9.  Turn the binding to the back of the quilt and hand sew it in place, using thread that matches the binding. Miter the corners as shown.

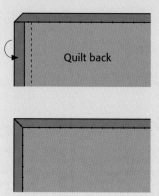

# Rails: Glo in the Dark

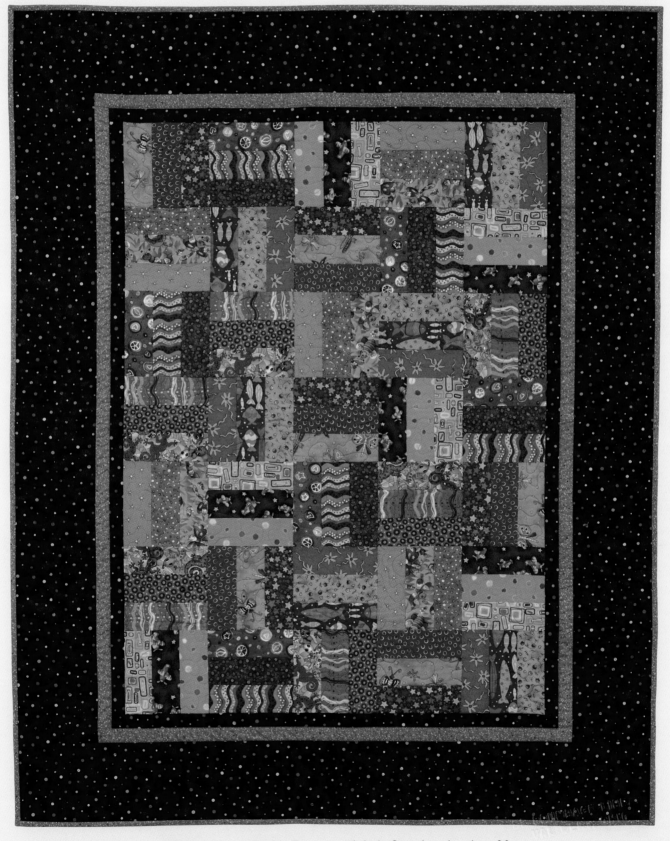

Made by Lynn Roddy Brown with help from her daughter Nancy

The fabrics in the quilt are all clear, bright prints, many with a juvenile theme. I chose medium to dark values without any white; I felt that white would dilute the intensity of the colors. There are touches of yellow in many of the prints but I did not use fabrics with yellow backgrounds because they were lighter in value than the other fabrics I chose. After sewing the blocks together, I first tried the pink print as an inner border next to the blocks, but I found that the dark purple gave a stronger line to clearly define the center of the quilt.

Finished quilt: 46½" x 58½"
Finished block: 6" x 6"

SKILL LEVELS

Piecing: Beginner
Fabric Selection: Easy

## Materials

*All yardages are based on 42"-wide fabric.*
+ 1½ yards of dark purple dot for inner and outer borders
+ ¾ yard of pink print for middle border and binding
+ 18 scrap strips, 5½" x 20", of different medium to dark bright prints for blocks
+ 3⅛ yards of fabric for backing
+ 54" x 66" piece of batting

## Cutting

**From the dark purple dot, cut:**
+ 4 strips, 1½" x 50", from the lengthwise grain
+ 4 strips, 6½" x 50", from the lengthwise grain

**From the pink print, cut:**
+ 5 strips, 1½" x 42"
+ 6 strips, 2½" x 42"

## Making the Blocks

Blocks are made in sets of six. For each set of blocks, you'll need:
+ 3 scrap strips of medium to dark bright prints (5½" x 20")

1. Cut each of the scrap strips into two 2½" x 20" strips as shown.

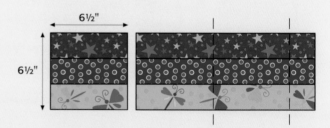

2. Sew three strips, one of each color, into a strip set. Sew the remaining three strips into a strip set, but arrange the colors in a different order. Press seams to one side. Trim and square up the left edge of each strip set; cut three 6½"-wide segments from each.

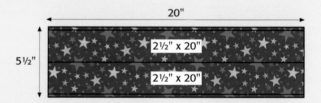

3. Repeat steps 1 and 2 until you've completed 36 blocks.

## Assembling the Quilt Top

1. Working on your design wall, arrange the blocks in seven horizontal rows of five blocks each, alternating the blocks horizontally and vertically. The blocks were made in groups of six, so be sure to scatter the blocks from each set across the surface of the quilt. You'll have one extra block.

2. Join the blocks to form rows. Press the seams toward the vertical blocks.

3. Join the rows, pressing the seams open.

4. Refer to "Adding Borders" on page 25. Add the purple inner borders, using the 1½" x 50" strips.

5. Refer to "Joining Border Strips" on page 25. Cut one of the 1½"-wide pink strips into two equal lengths. Using a diagonal seam, sew these half strips to the ends of full-length strips. Press the seam open. Add the pink side borders.

6. Add the pink top and bottom borders, using a 1½"-wide strip for each.

7. Add the purple outer borders, using the 6½" x 50" strips.

## Finishing the Quilt

1. Cut the backing fabric, across the grain, into two equal pieces. Remove the selvages. Sew these pieces together along the lengthwise grain and press the seam open to create the quilt back. The seam will run horizontally across the quilt.

2. Refer to "Layering and Basting" on page 26.

3. Hand or machine quilt as desired.

4. Refer to "Binding" on page 27 and use the pink 2½"-wide strips to bind the quilt.

5. Make and attach a label to your quilt.

# Rails: Love to Mary

Pieced by Lynn Roddy Brown, Janice Thompson, and the Piecemakers of Bellaire United Methodist Church.
Hand quilted and finished by Mary Tomlinson.

My Friday quilt group made this Signature quilt for one of our members who moved away. We chose the pattern because it's easy to piece and had room for each of us to sign our names in the block centers. The fabrics we chose are mostly Civil War–reproduction prints of medium to dark value. If you're making the blocks for a Signature quilt, choose a light fabric for the center strip. This will form a strong contrast within the blocks and allow the signatures to show up nicely.

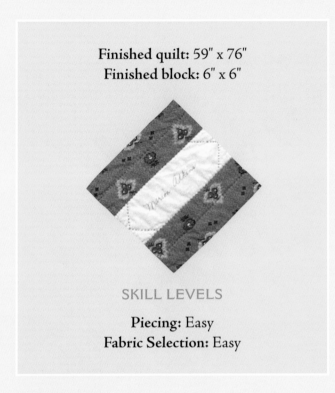

**Finished quilt: 59" x 76"**
**Finished block: 6" x 6"**

SKILL LEVELS

**Piecing:** Easy
**Fabric Selection:** Easy

## Materials

*All yardages are based on 42"-wide fabric unless otherwise noted.*

- 2 yards of brown print for outer border
- 1 yard of gold print for setting triangles
- ⅞ yard of cream print for blocks
- ⅝ yard of red print for inner border
- 20 scrap strips, 5½" x 20", of different medium to dark prints for blocks
- ⅔ yard of light brown print for binding
- 5⅛ yards of fabric for backing
- 67" x 84" piece of batting
- Plastic-coated freezer paper
- Fine-point Pigma pen in brown or black

## Cutting

**From the cream print, cut:**
- 10 strips, 2½" x 42"; crosscut into 20 strips, 2½" x 20"

**From the gold print, cut:**
- 2 strips, 11" x 42"; crosscut into 5 squares, 11" x 11". Cut each square twice diagonally to yield 20 side triangles.
- 2 squares, 6½" x 6½". Cut each square once diagonally to yield 4 corner triangles.

**From the red print, cut:**
- 7 strips, 2½" x 42"

**From the brown print, cut:**
- 4 strips, 6½" x 68", from the lengthwise grain

**From the light brown print, cut:**
- 7 strips, 2½" x 42"

## Making the Blocks

Blocks are made in sets of three. For each set of blocks, you'll need:
- 1 scrap strip of medium to dark print (5½" x 20")
- 1 cream strip (2½" x 20")

1. Cut the scrap strip into two strips, 2½" x 20", as shown.

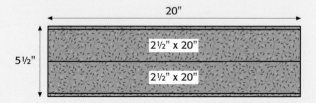

2. Sew the medium/dark strips to each side of the cream strip. Press the seams toward the medium/dark. Trim and square up the left edge; cut three segments, 6½" wide.

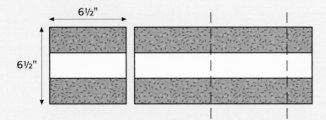

3. Repeat steps 1 and 2 until you've completed 60 blocks.

## Signing Made Easy

To make writing the signatures easier, use freezer paper to stabilize the fabric. Cut the freezer paper into 2" x 6" strips and iron, shiny side down, to the back of the block centers. Use a fine-point Pigma pen for the signatures. Gently remove the freezer paper before sewing the top together.

## Assembling the Quilt Top

1. Working on a design wall and referring to the quilt diagram, arrange the blocks, setting triangles, and corner triangles in a diagonal set. Be sure to scatter the identical blocks across the surface of the quilt. You'll have one extra block.

2. Referring to "Diagonal Sets" on page 24, sew the side-setting triangles and blocks together into diagonal rows. Press the seams as shown in the quilt diagram.

Quilt diagram

3. Join the rows. Press the seams open. Add the corner triangles.

4. Referring to "Diagonal Sets," trim the quilt so that you have a ¼" seam allowance on the outside edges.

5. Refer to "Joining Border Strips" on page 25. For each of the red side borders, use two 2½"-wide strips. Sew these strips end to end, using a diagonal seam. Press this seam open. Referring to "Adding Borders" on page 25, add the side inner borders.

6. To make the top and bottom inner borders, cut one of the 2½"-wide red strips into two equal lengths. Using a diagonal seam, sew these half strips to the ends of full-length strips. Press the seam open. Add the top and bottom inner borders.

7. Add the brown outer borders, using the 6½"x 68" strips.

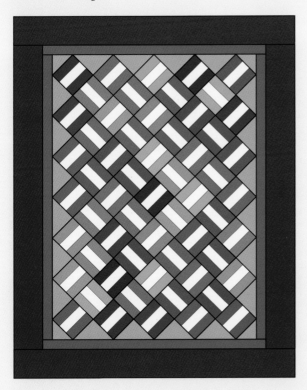

## Finishing the Quilt

1. Cut the backing fabric, across the grain, into two equal pieces. Remove the selvages. Sew these pieces together along the lengthwise grain to create the quilt back. Press the seam open. The seam will run vertically on the quilt.

2. Refer to "Layering and Basting" on page 26.

3. Hand or machine quilt as desired.

4. Refer to "Binding" on page 27 and use the light brown 2½"-wide strips to bind the quilt.

5. Make and attach a label to your quilt.

# Bars: A Little Bit of Everything

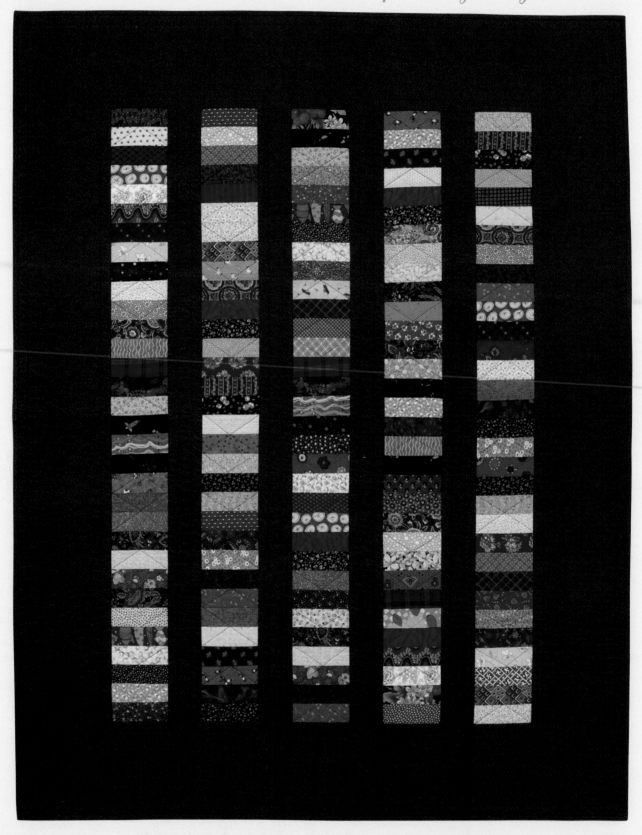

Made by Lynn Roddy Brown with help from her daughter Nancy

Here's an ideal quilt to use up odds and ends. It was made from leftover pieces from other quilts in this book. I threw in a few other scraps from my sewing room as well. This quilt works because there are several pieces of everything. If there were only one piece of 1930s fabric or one piece of bright, they would stand out from the rest.

I originally bought the border and binding fabric on sale to be used as a backing. I decided it was too boring even for backing. When this quilt was in progress on the design wall, there was so much happening that dark, plain, and boring became the perfect complement.

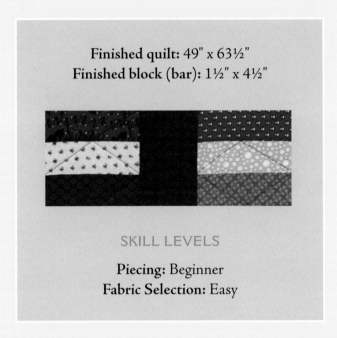

**Finished quilt:** 49" x 63½"
**Finished block (bar):** 1½" x 4½"

SKILL LEVELS

**Piecing:** Beginner
**Fabric Selection:** Easy

## Materials

*All yardages are based on 42"-wide fabric unless other-wise noted.*

- 2⅞ yards of dark gray print for borders and binding
- 160 pieces, 2" x 5½", of different fabrics for bars*
- 3½ yards of fabric for backing
- 57" x 72" piece of batting

*These pieces could be cut from 18 scrap strips (5½" x 20"). Related fabrics would probably be a better choice for this option since each fabric would be used nine times.*

## Cutting

**From the dark gray print, cut;**
- 6 strips, 2½" x 42"
- 6 strips, 3¼" x 42"
- 4 strips, 8" x 56", cut from the lengthwise grain

## Making the Panels

1. You should have 160 pieces, 2" x 5½", of assorted fabrics. If you're using 5½" x 20" scrap strips, cut as shown.

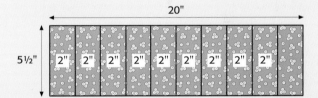

2. Join the pieces in groups of three or four along the 5½" sides. Place these on the design wall in five rows of 32 pieces each. Arrange them until you're satisfied with the placement.

3. Join the pieces into five panels of 32 units each. Press the seams in the same direction. Measure the rows. They must all be the same length. Make adjustments if necessary.

4. To make certain you have an even edge, carefully trim ⅛" or less from one side of the pieced strips. Rotate the strip and make a second cut to the opposite side, making the pieced strips 5" wide.

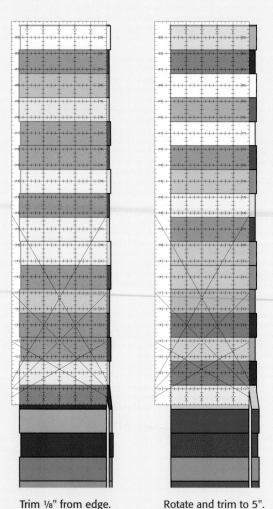

Trim ⅛" from edge.    Rotate and trim to 5".

## Assembling the Quilt Top

1. To make the four vertical sashing strips, cut two of the 3¼"-wide strips into two equal lengths. Using a straight seam, sew each of the half strips to the end of a full-length strip. Referring to "Vertical Strippy Sets" on page 23, cut the sashing strips the length of the panels and join the sashing strips and panels.

2. Referring to "Adding Borders" on page 25, add the 8" x 56" gray border strips to the sides, top, and bottom.

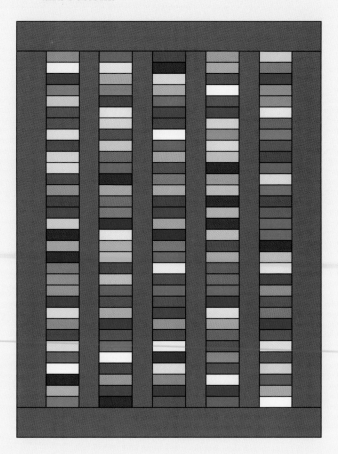

## Finishing the Quilt

1. Cut the backing fabric, across the grain, into two equal pieces. Remove the selvages. Sew the pieces together along the lengthwise grain to create the back. Press this seam open. The seam will run horizontally across the quilt.

2. Refer to "Layering and Basting" on page 26.

3. Hand or machine quilt as desired.

4. Referring to "Binding" on page 27, use the 2½"-wide gray strips to bind the quilt.

5. Make and attach a label to your quilt.

# Bars: Almost All My Plaids

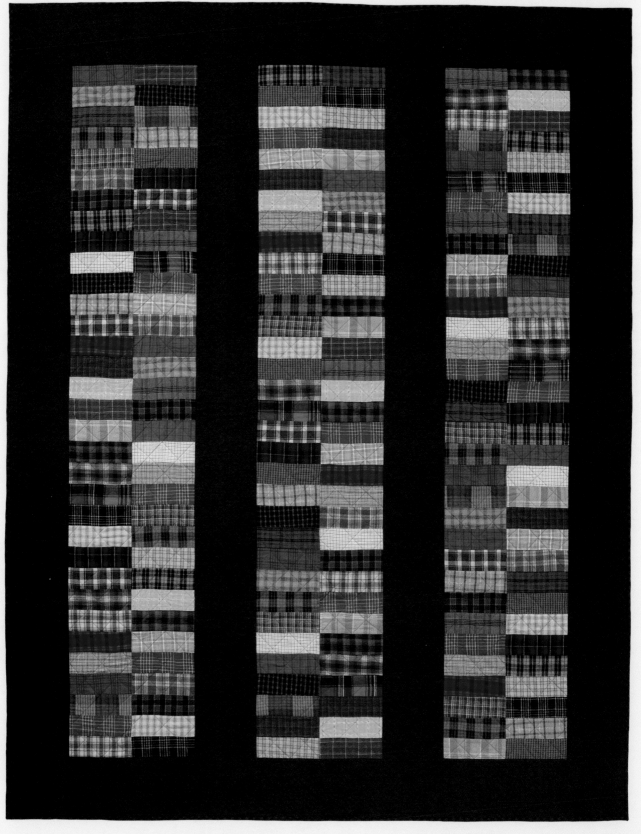

Made by Lynn Roddy Brown with help from her daughter Nancy

I designed this quilt to use 33 different plaids. When I went to my stash, I had no problem finding the number I needed. This will give you some idea of the scope of my stash. The plaids were collected several years ago and not used until I created this quilt for the book. You never know what fabrics you're going to need or when, so my advice is to just buy some of everything! The almost-solid dark green fabric used in the vertical sashing and border provides a strong contrast. It allows the plaids to take center stage.

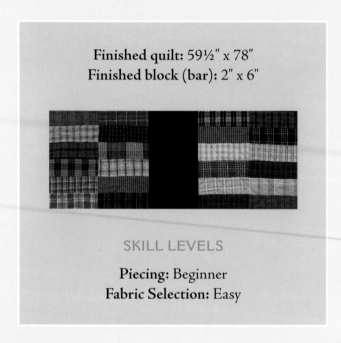

Finished quilt: 59½" x 78"
Finished block (bar): 2" x 6"

SKILL LEVELS

Piecing: Beginner
Fabric Selection: Easy

## Materials

*All yardages are based on 42"-wide fabric unless otherwise noted.*

+ 2⅝ yards of dark green print for sashing and borders
+ 33 scrap strips, 5½" x 20", of different plaids for bars
+ ⅔ yard of dark green plaid for binding*
+ 5¼ yards of fabric for backing
+ 68" x 86" piece of batting

*For bias binding, you'll need 1 yard to make a 287" length.*

## Cutting

*Do not cut sashing and borders until the pieced rows are complete.*

**From the dark green print, cut:**
+ 6 strips, 6¼" x 70", from the lengthwise grain*

**From the dark green plaid, cut:**
+ 8 strips, 2½" x 42" (for straight-grain binding)

*If you can cut only 5 strips from the lengthwise grain, cut 2 strips crosswise, 6¼" x 42", and piece them for the bottom border.*

## Making the Panels

1. Cut 6 pieces, 2½" x 6½", from each of the 33 plaid scrap strips (5½" x 20") as shown.

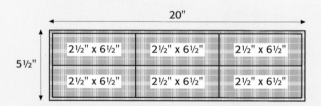

2. Join the 2½" x 6½" pieces into random groups of three or four along the 6½" sides. Place these on the design wall in six vertical rows of 33 pieces each. Arrange the rows in pairs until they're pleasing to you.

3. Join all the pieces into vertical rows. Press the seams of the first row in each group up, and the seams of the second row in each group down. Measure the rows. If they're not all the same length, make adjustments.

4. Join the rows into three groups of two each, carefully matching the opposing seams. Pin the seams. Sew the pieced rows together and press the seams open.

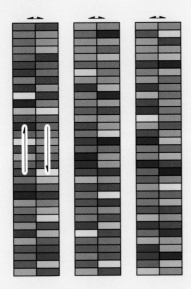

## Assembling the Quilt Top

1. Referring to "Vertical Strippy Sets" on page 23, measure the rows and cut the two print sashing strips. Sew the seams to join the pieced rows together.

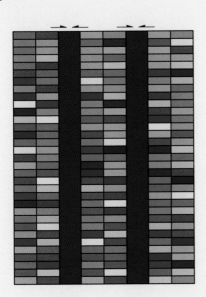

2. Refer to "Adding Borders" on page 25. Add the side borders and then the top and bottom, piecing the bottom border strip if necessary.

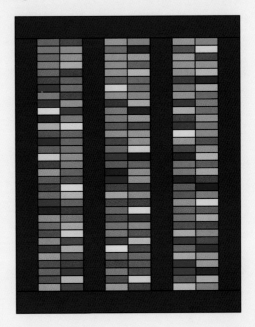

## Finishing the Quilt

1. Cut the backing fabric, across the grain, into two equal pieces. Remove the selvages. Sew these pieces together along the lengthwise grain to create the back. Press this seam open. The seam will run vertically on the quilt.

2. Refer to "Layering and Basting" on page 26.

3. Hand or machine quilt as desired.

4. Refer to "Binding" on page 27 and use the plaid 2½"-wide strips to bind the quilt.

5. Make and attach a label to your quilt.

# Puss in a Corner: Nana's Scrap Quilt

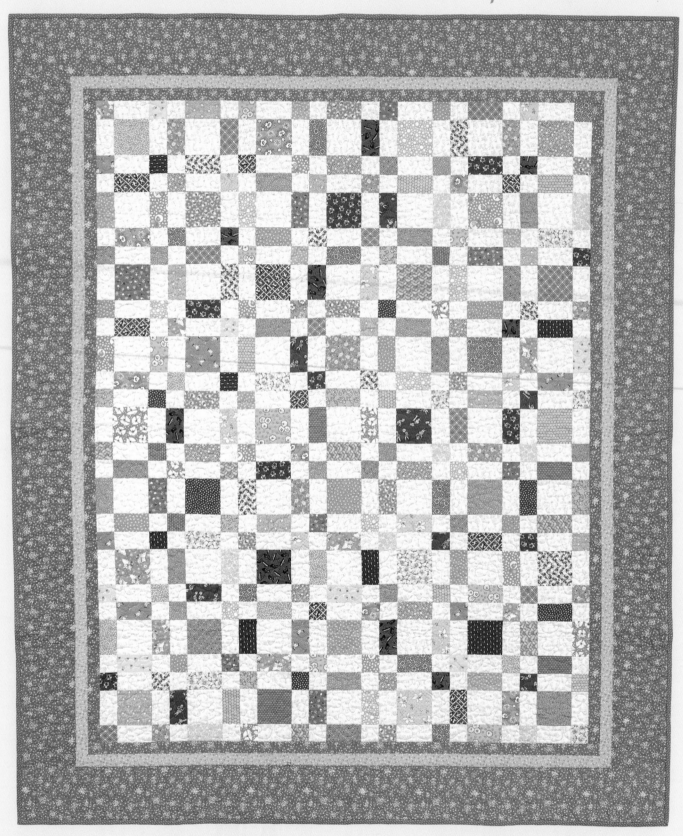

Made by Lynn Roddy Brown with help from her daughter Nancy

This quilt was made using 1930s-reproduction prints against a background of very light blue-and-white print. Muslin would also be a good background choice. Just make sure there is strong contrast between the background and the prints. The print in the medium blue border fabric is less busy than most of the fabrics used in the body of the quilt. This gives contrast and helps frame the blocks.

**Finished quilt: 56½" x 68½"**
**Finished block: 6" x 6"**

### SKILL LEVELS

**Piecing: Beginner**
**Fabric Selection: Easy**

## Materials

*All yardages are based on 42"-wide fabric unless otherwise noted.*

✦ 2⅛ yards of light blue-and-white print for blocks
✦ 2 yards of medium blue print for inner and outer borders
✦ ⅜ yard of yellow print for middle border
✦ 35 scrap strips, 5½" x 20", of different medium to dark 1930s-reproduction prints for blocks
✦ ⅔ yard of green print for binding
✦ 4 yards of fabric for backing
✦ 65" x 77" piece of batting

## Cutting

**From the light blue-and-white print, cut:**
✦ 8 strips, 8½" x 42"; crosscut into 35 rectangles, 3½" x 8½", and 70 rectangles, 2" x 8½"

**From the yellow print, cut:**
✦ 6 strips, 1½" x 42"

**From the medium blue print, cut:**
✦ 4 strips, 5½" x 62", from the lengthwise grain
✦ 4 strips, 1½" x 62", from the lengthwise grain

**From the green print, cut:**
✦ 7 strips, 2½" x 42"

## Making the Blocks

The blocks are made in sets of 10, using five reproduction fabrics. I used five different colors for each set; this helps scatter the colors across the surface of the quilt. Each set consists of five A blocks and five B blocks. You'll need 63 blocks. I made 70 and then chose the ones I liked best. Use the extra seven blocks as part of the quilt backing, or use them in pillows or pillowcases.

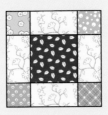
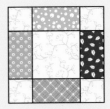

Block A          Block B

**For each set of blocks, you'll need:**

✦ 5 scrap strips of medium to dark 1930s-reproduction prints (5½" x 20")

✦ 5 rectangles, 3½" x 8½", of light blue–and-white print

✦ 10 rectangles, 2" x 8½", of light blue–and-white print

1. Cut each of the five 1930s prints into one rectangle, 3½" x 8½", and two rectangles, 2" x 8½", as shown. From the scraps, cut a piece, approximately 1" x 1", of each fabric; this will be used in step 3.

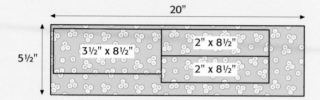

2. Following the diagrams, make five strip sets, using the five print 3½" x 8½" pieces cut in step 1 and 10 blue-and-white 2" x 8½" pieces. Press toward the reproduction prints. Cut each of the five strip sets into one 3½"-wide segment and two 2"-wide segments.

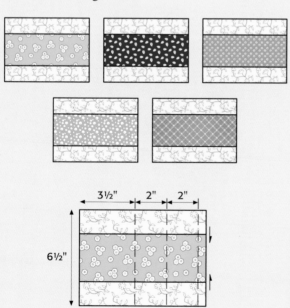

3. Assign a number to each of the five 1" scraps cut in step 1. Lay out five 3½" x 8½" blue-and-white strips. Place the 2" x 8½" colored strips on each side in the order shown. *Each strip set must use two different 1930s fabrics and each strip set should be different.* Carefully check the fabric placements and sew the strip sets. Press toward the reproduction prints. From each strip set, cut one 3½"-wide segment and two 2"-wide segments.

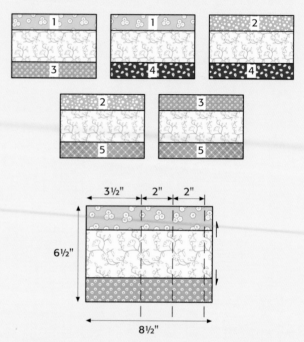

4. Sort the segments cut in steps 2 and 3 into 5 A blocks and 5 B blocks. Each A block should have five different fabrics. Each B block should have four different fabrics. Don't sew any blocks until all the segments have been sorted.

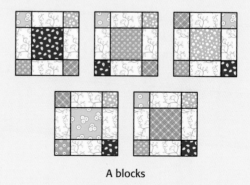

A blocks

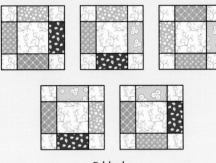

B blocks

5. Sew the block pieces together in rows. Press the block A seams outward. Press the block B seams inward.

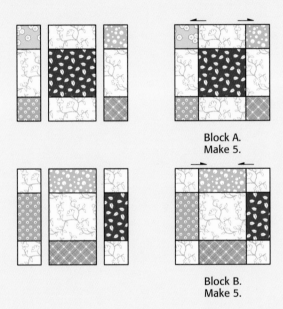

Block A.
Make 5.

Block B.
Make 5.

6. Repeat steps 1–5 until you've completed 70 blocks, 35 each of block A and block B.

## Assembling the Quilt Top

1. Study the quilt diagram at right and the photograph on page 42. There are nine horizontal rows with seven blocks in each row. The A and B blocks alternate from row to row, with the top row beginning and ending with an A block. As you place the blocks on the design wall, scatter the blocks of each set across the surface. You'll use 32 A blocks and 31 B blocks; there will be seven extra blocks.

2. Sew the horizontal rows together. Press the seams open.

3. Join the rows. Press the seams open.

4. Refer to "Adding Borders" on page 25. Add the medium blue inner borders, using the 1½" x 62" strips.

5. Refer to "Joining Border Strips" on page 25. Cut two of the yellow 1½"-wide strips into two equal lengths. Using a diagonal seam, sew each of these half strips to the end of a full-length strip. Add the yellow borders.

6. Add the medium blue outer borders, using the 5½" x 62" strips.

Quilt diagram

## Finishing the Quilt

1. Cut the backing fabric, across the grain, into two equal pieces. Remove the selvages. Sew these pieces together along the lengthwise grain to create the quilt back. Press the seam open. The seam will run horizontally across the quilt.

2. Refer to "Layering and Basting" on page 26.

3. Hand or machine quilt as desired.

4. Refer to "Binding" on page 27 and use the green 2½"-wide strips to bind the quilt.

5. Make and attach a label to your quilt.

# Puss in a Corner: Orange Blossom Special

Made by Lynn Roddy Brown

This quilt was made from traded blocks. When my husband saw the quilt, he named it after one of his favorite Western tunes.

My original plan was to use a variety of teal fabrics for the setting triangles. This required a shopping trip. I bought six different teals; I also bought a lovely medium blue floral from the sale table. When I got home, I discovered that the teal fabrics overpowered the quilt, but the sale-table blue was perfect. The yellow inner border came from my stash. It has touches of blue and reddish orange. I never planned to make a quilt with a reddish orange border. Sometimes things just happen.

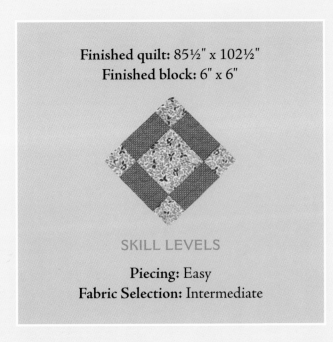

Finished quilt: 85½" x 102½"
Finished block: 6" x 6"

SKILL LEVELS

Piecing: Easy
Fabric Selection: Intermediate

## Materials

*All yardages are based on 42"-wide fabric unless otherwise noted.*

+ 2⅞ yards of reddish orange print for outer border
+ 1⅓ yards of blue floral print for setting triangles
+ ⅝ yard of yellow print for inner border
+ 72 scrap strips, 5½" x 20", of different light prints for blocks
+ 72 scrap strips, 5½" x 20", of different medium to dark prints for blocks
+ ⅞ yard of blue textured print for binding
+ 8⅔ yards of fabric for backing
+ 94" x 111" piece of batting

## Cutting

**From the blue floral print, cut:**
+ 3 strips, 11" x 42"; crosscut strips into 8 squares, 11" x 11"; cut each square twice diagonally to yield 32 side triangles
+ 2 squares, 6½" x 6½"; cut each square once diagonally to yield 4 corner triangles

**From the yellow print, cut:**
+ 9 strips, 2" x 42"

**From the reddish orange print, cut:**
+ 4 strips, 7½" x 92", from the lengthwise grain

**From the blue textured print, cut:**
+ 10 strips, 2½" x 42"

## Making the Blocks

For this quilt, you'll need 80 of block A and 63 of block B. Follow the directions below to make 63 sets of two, composed of one A block and one B block; then make 18 of block A in pairs as instructed.

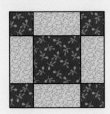

Block A.
Make 80.

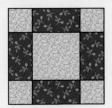

Block B.
Make 63.

**For each set of blocks, you'll need:**

✦   1 scrap strip of medium to dark print
    (5½" x 20")
✦   1 scrap strip of light print (5½" x 20")

## MAKING SETS OF A AND B BLOCKS

1.  Cut each of the two strips into one 3½" x 8½"
    rectangle and two 2" x 8½" rectangles as shown.

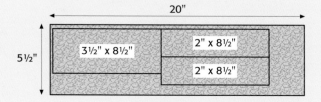

2.  Make two strip sets as shown. Press toward the
    medium to dark fabric. From each strip set, cut
    one 3½"-wide segment and two 2"-wide segments.

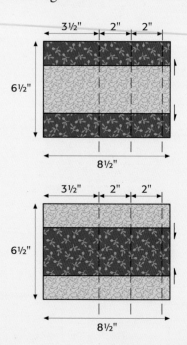

3.  Arrange the segments to make one A block and
    one B block. Sew the rows of each block. Press

the seams away from the center of block A and
toward the center of block B.

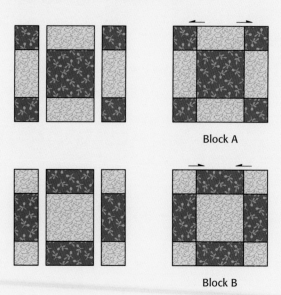

Block A

Block B

4.  Repeat steps 1–3 until you've completed 63
    pairs of blocks.

## MAKING PAIRS OF A BLOCKS

1. Cut each of the two strips into one 3½" x 8½" rectangle and two 2" x 8½" strips as you did in step 1 of "Making Sets of A and B Blocks."

2. Make two strip sets as shown. Press toward the medium to dark fabric. From strip set X, cut four 2"-wide segments. From strip set Y, cut two 3½"-wide segments.

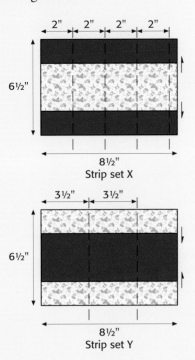

8½"
Strip set X

8½"
Strip set Y

3. Arrange the segments to make two A blocks. Sew the rows of each block and press the seams away from the center.

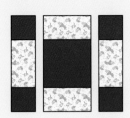 

Block A.
Make 2.

4. Repeat steps 1–3 until you've completed nine pairs of A blocks.

## Assembling the Quilt Top

1. Working on a design wall and referring to the quilt diagram, arrange the blocks, setting triangles, and corner triangles in a diagonal set. Note the positions of the A and B blocks. Be sure to separate blocks using the same fabrics. You'll have one extra A block.

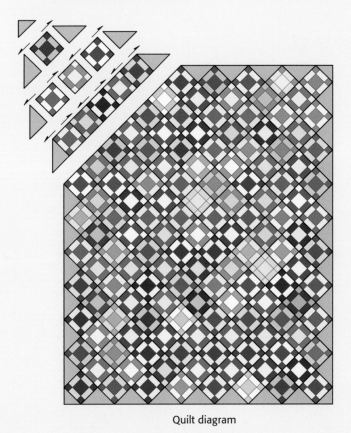

Quilt diagram

2. Referring to "Diagonal Sets" on page 24, sew the side-setting triangles and blocks together into diagonal rows. Press the seams open.

3. Join the rows. Press the seams open. Add the corner triangles.

4. Referring to "Diagonal Sets," trim the quilt so that you have a ¼" seam allowance on the outside edges.

5. Refer to "Joining Border Strips" on page 25. For each of the yellow side inner borders, first sew two 2"-wide strips end to end, using a diagonal seam. Cut an additional yellow strip into two equal lengths. Sew these half strips to the ends of the side inner borders. Press the seams open. Refer to "Adding Borders" on page 25 and add the side inner borders.

6. For each of the top and bottom inner borders, sew two 2"-wide yellow strips together using a diagonal seam. Press the seams open. Add the top and bottom inner borders.

7. Add the reddish orange outer borders, using the 7½" x 92" strips.

## Finishing the Quilt

1. Cut the backing fabric, across the grain, into three equal pieces. Remove the selvages. Sew these pieces together along the lengthwise grain to create the quilt back. Press the seams open. The seams will run horizontally across the quilt.

2. Refer to "Layering and Basting" on page 26.

3. Hand or machine quilt as desired.

4. Refer to "Binding" on page 27 and use the 2½"-wide blue strips to bind the quilt.

5. Make and attach a label to your quilt.

# Double Four Patch: Mad about Purple and Plaid

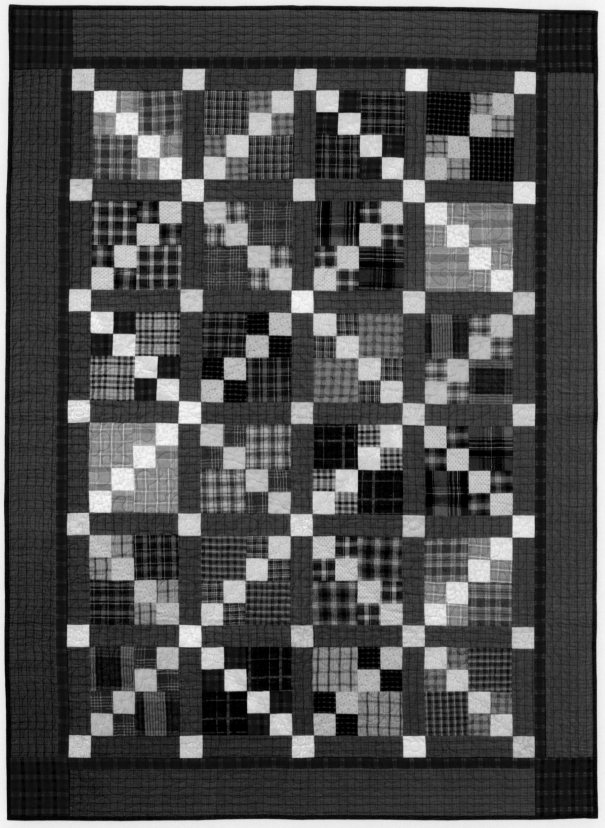

Made by Lynn Roddy Brown with help from her daughter Nancy

I delved into my collection of plaids to make this quilt. I found a purple plaid for the sashing and border that has less texture than the other plaids in the quilt. This helps contain all the busyness in the blocks.

The plaid blocks, sewn together with the purple plaid sashing, were on my design wall for three weeks before I could make a decision about the borders. I was even forced to shop (how dreadful!), and several pieces of fabric reside in my stash as a result of that trip. Finally, I noticed a tiny red line in the purple plaid. This helped determine the inner border. I had a limited amount of purple plaid, which explains the slightly narrow outer border and red corner squares. Sometimes, not having enough fabric is a good thing—it forces you to make decisions you wouldn't have made otherwise.

**Finished quilt: 53½" x 73½"**
**Finished block: 8" x 8"**

SKILL LEVELS

**Piecing:** Beginner
**Fabric Selection:** Easy

## Materials

*All yardages are based on 42"-wide fabric unless otherwise noted.*

+ 2½ yards of purple plaid for outer border and sashing
+ ⅝ yard of red plaid for inner border and corner squares
+ 18 scrap strips, 5½" x 20", of different medium to dark plaid for blocks
+ 12 scrap strips, 5½" x 20", of different beige prints for blocks and sashing squares
+ ⅝ yard of dark purple fabric for binding
+ 4 yards of fabric for backing
+ 62" x 82" piece of batting

## Cutting

**From the purple plaid, cut:**
+ 4 strips, 5" x 72", from the lengthwise grain
+ From the remainder, cut 58 strips, 2½" x 8½"*

**From the red plaid, cut:**
+ 7 strips, 1½" x 42"
+ 4 squares, 6" x 6"

**From the dark purple fabric, cut:**
+ 7 strips, 2½" x 42"

*Wait until the blocks have been completed before cutting the sashing strips.*

## Making the Blocks

The blocks are made in sets of four. For each set of blocks, you'll need:
+ 3 scrap strips of medium to dark plaid (5½" x 20")
+ 2 scrap strips of beige prints (5½" x 20")

1.  From each of the beige strips, cut one rectangle 5½" x 10½". Set the leftover beige pieces aside. They will be used for sashing squares.

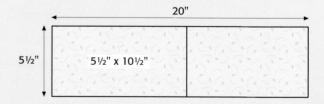

2. Cut two of the plaid strips into one 5½" x 10½" rectangle and two 4½" squares as shown.

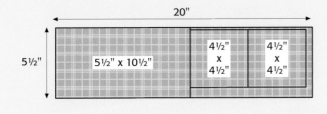

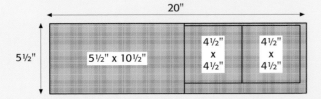

3. Cut the remaining plaid strip into four 4½" squares.

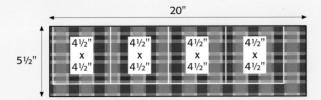

4. Referring to "Constructing Units from Paired Fabrics" on page 18, pair each of the beige 5½" x 10½" rectangles with a plaid 5½" x 10½" rectangle. Cut each set of paired fabrics into four 2½" x 5½" segments. Refer to "Four-Patch Units" on page 19. Make eight four-patch units.

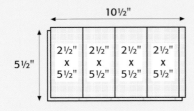

5. Arrange the eight four-patch units made in step 4 and the eight 4½" squares cut in steps 2 and 3 into four blocks, varying the fabric placement in each as shown. Make certain the light fabric of the four-patch units is positioned correctly.

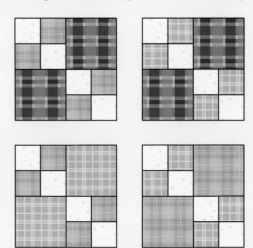

6. Sew the pieces of each block together in rows and press the seams toward the unpieced squares. Sew the rows together and press the seams open.

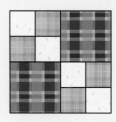

7.  Repeat steps 1–6 until you've completed 24 blocks.

8.  Measure the blocks. They should be 8½" x 8½"; however, if they vary, use your measurement to cut the purple plaid sashing strips to match the blocks.

9.  Use the beige fabric set aside in step 1 to cut 35 sashing squares, 2½" square.

## Assembling the Quilt Top

1.  Following the quilt diagram, arrange the blocks on your design wall in six horizontal rows of four blocks each. Keep in mind that the blocks were made in sets. Scatter the blocks of each set across the surface. Turn the blocks until the four-patch units form diagonal lines. Add the purple sashing strips and beige sashing squares to the design wall.

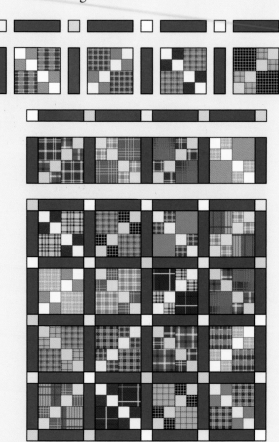

Quilt diagram

2.  Sew the horizontal rows of blocks and sashing strips together. Press toward the sashing.

3.  Sew the horizontal rows of sashing strips and sashing squares together. Press toward the sashing.

4.  Join the rows. Press toward the sashing.

5.  Refer to "Joining Border Strips" on page 25. For each of the red side inner borders, use two 1½"-wide strips. Sew these strips end to end, using a straight seam. Press this seam open. To make the top and bottom inner borders, cut one of the 1½"-wide red strips into two equal lengths. Using a straight seam, sew these half strips to the ends of full-length strips. Press the seam open.

6.  Sew the red inner borders to the purple plaid 5" x 72" strips for the outer border. Press toward the inner border.

7.  Refer to "Adding Borders" on page 25. Measure the quilt through the middle lengthwise and crosswise. Use the lengthwise measurement to cut the pieced side borders; use the crosswise measurement to cut the top and bottom pieced borders.

8.  Sew the two side borders to the quilt. Press toward the borders.

### Cutting Plaids

For scrap quilts, I do not align the plaids when cutting. Slightly off-grain patches add more energy to a quilt.

9. Sew the red corner squares to each end of the top and bottom borders. Press toward the borders. Add the top and bottom borders to the quilt. Press the seams toward the borders.

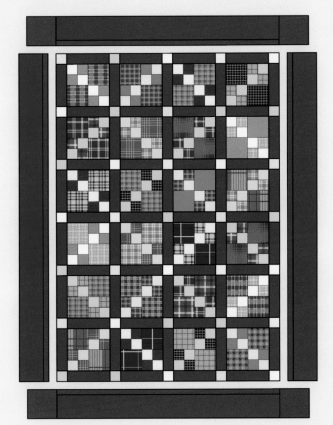

## Finishing the Quilt

1. Cut the backing fabric, across the grain, into two equal pieces. Remove the selvages. Sew these pieces together along the lengthwise grain to create the quilt back. Press the seam open. The seam will run horizontally across the quilt.

2. Refer to "Layering and Basting" on page 26.

3. Hand or machine quilt as desired.

4. Refer to "Binding" on page 27 and use the dark purple 2½"-wide strips to bind the quilt.

5. Make and attach a label to your quilt.

# Double Four Patch: Echoing Squares

Made by Lynn Roddy Brown with help from her daughter Nancy

The fabrics used in this quilt are Civil War–reproduction prints along with other fabrics in similar shades, giving it an appealing old-fashioned flavor. The four-patch units that form the chains are made using the same light beige fabric in all the blocks. To create a distinct diagonal chain, the light fabric needs to have high contrast with the other fabrics used in the blocks.

The width of the stripe repeat determined the width of the borders. You may need to alter the width of the border based on the stripe you choose.

Finished quilt: 82½" x 98½"
Finished block: 8" x 8"

SKILL LEVELS

Piecing: Beginner
Fabric Selection: Easy

## Materials

*All yardages are based on 42"-wide fabric unless otherwise noted.*
+ 2⅞ yards of brown stripe for outer border
+ 2 yards of beige print for four-patch units
+ 1⅜ yards of burgundy print for inner border and binding
+ 60 scrap strips, 5½" x 20", of different medium to dark prints for blocks
+ 8¼ yards of fabric for backing
+ 91" x 107" piece of batting

## Cutting

**From the beige print, cut:**
+ 6 strips, 10½" x 42"; crosscut into 40 rectangles, 5½" x 10½"

**From the burgundy print, cut:**
+ 9 strips, 1½" x 42"
+ 10 strips, 2½" x 42"

**From the brown stripe, cut:**
+ 4 strips, 8½" x 94", from the lengthwise grain*

*\*You may need to cut your border slightly wider or narrower, depending on the width of the stripe repeat of your fabric. Refer to "Fussy Cutting Stripes" on page 59.*

## Making the Blocks

Blocks are made in sets of four. For each set of blocks, you'll need:
+ 3 scrap strips of medium to dark prints (5½" x 20")
+ 2 beige rectangles, 5½" x 10½"

1. Cut two of the medium to dark scrap strips into one 5½" x 10½" rectangle and two 4½" squares as shown.

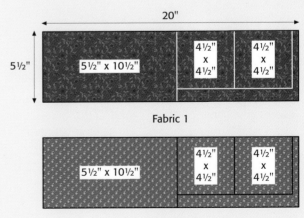

Fabric 1

Fabric 2

2. Cut the remaining medium to dark strip into four 4½" squares.

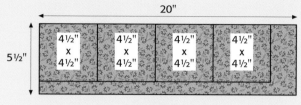

Fabric 3

3. Referring to "Constructing Units from Paired Fabrics" on page 18, pair each of the beige 5½" x 10½" rectangles with a medium to dark 5½" x 10½" rectangle. Cut each set of paired fabrics into four 2½" x 5½" segments as shown. Refer to "Four-Patch Units" on page 19 to make eight four-patch units.

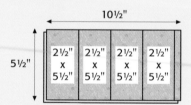

4. Arrange the eight four-patch units made in step 3 and the eight 4½" squares cut in steps 1 and 2 into four blocks, varying the placement of the fabrics as shown. Make certain the beige fabric in each four-patch unit is positioned correctly.

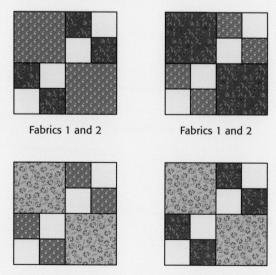

Fabrics 1 and 2       Fabrics 1 and 2

Fabrics 1 and 3       Fabrics 2 and 3

5. Sew the pieces together in rows and press the seams toward the unpieced squares. Sew the rows together and press the seams open.

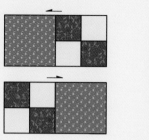

6. Repeat steps 1–5 until you've completed 80 blocks.

## Assembling the Quilt Top

1. The blocks were made in sets of four. Divide the quilt into four quarters, and using a design wall, place one block from a set in each quarter. Following the quilt diagram, arrange the blocks in each quarter into five horizontal rows of four blocks each. Turn the blocks to create the diagonal lines.

Quilt diagram

2. Sew the blocks of each quarter into horizontal rows. Press the seams open.

3. Join the rows in each quarter. Press the seams open.

4. Join the quarters to complete the top.

5. Refer to "Joining Border Strips" on page 25. For each of the burgundy side inner borders, first sew two 1½"-wide strips end to end, using a diagonal seam. Cut an additional burgundy strip into two equal lengths. Sew these half strips to the ends of the side inner borders. Press the seams open. Refer to "Adding Borders" on page 25 to add the side inner borders.

6. For the top and bottom inner borders, sew two 1½"-wide burgundy strips end to end, using a diagonal seam. Make two. Press the seams open. Add the top and bottom inner borders.

7. Add the striped outer border, using the 8½" x 94" strips.

## Finishing the Quilt

1. Cut the backing fabric, across the grain, into three equal pieces. Remove the selvages. Sew these pieces together along the lengthwise grain to create the quilt back. Press the seams open. The seams will run horizontally across the quilt.

2. Refer to "Layering and Basting" on page 26.

3. Hand or machine quilt as desired.

4. Refer to "Binding" on page 27 and use the burgundy 2½"-wide strips to bind the quilt.

5. Make and attach a label to your quilt.

### Fussy Cutting Stripes

To fussy cut a lengthwise stripe, first study the fabric to find one stripe or a combination of stripes that will approximately equal the desired width. For "Down the Line" on page 60, I had a 1½"-wide finished inner border in mind. However, since the stripe I chose was 1⅛", I cut my strips at 1⅝", resulting in a narrower inner border and a slightly smaller quilt. When you've selected the stripe, you must add a ¼" seam allowance to each side. Lay the ¼" line of a rotary ruler on the line of the stripe you're using. Cut one layer at a time. Using a short ruler and realigning often seems to work best. Turn the fabric and add a ¼" seam to the other edge of the stripe.

When sewing the stripe to the quilt, place the stripe fabric on top. On the wrong side of the fabric, you should be able to see the stripe. Use the line in the fabric as a sewing line. It's more important visually to follow the stripe so that it won't be wavy or cut off on the right side of the quilt.

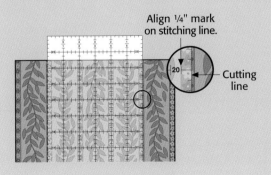

Align ¼" mark on stitching line.

Cutting line

# Texas Two-Step: Down the Line

Made by Lynn Roddy Brown. Block designed by Jackie Theriot.

The blocks for this quilt were made from traded four-patch and half-square-triangle units. The blues range from light to dark with some leaning toward teal. The yellows vary from light yellow to gold. Several of the fabrics have other colors in small amounts. Having a wide variety of blues and yellows adds interest to the quilt.

It took a long time to find an inner border that would contrast with the blocks. I had a wonderful blue-and-yellow plaid that, to my surprise, didn't work. Finally, I found the light blue stripe in my stash.

Finished quilt: 55½" x 71½"
Finished block: 8" x 8"

SKILL LEVELS

**Piecing:** Intermediate
**Fabric Selection:** Easy

## Materials

*All yardages are based on 42"-wide fabric unless otherwise noted.*

+ 2⅝ yards of medium blue print for outer border and binding
+ 1⅞ yards of light blue stripe for inner border*
+ 28 scrap strips, 5½" x 20", of different yellow prints for blocks
+ 28 scrap strips, 5½" x 20", of different blue prints for blocks
+ 4 yards of fabric for backing
+ 64" x 80" piece of batting

*One-half yard of light blue is sufficient for the inner border if using crosswise cuts. I cut the stripe on the lengthwise grain.*

## Cutting

**From the light blue stripe, cut:**
+ 6 strips, 2" x 42"**

**From the medium blue print, cut:**
+ 4 strips, 6½" x 64", from the lengthwise grain
+ 7 strips, 2½" x 42", from the crosswise grain

***Refer to the box "Fussy Cutting Stripes" on page 59 if you're using a lengthwise stripe.*

## Making the Blocks

Blocks are made in sets of four. For each set of blocks, you'll need:
+ 4 scrap strips of different yellow prints (5½" x 20")
+ 4 scrap strips of different blue prints (5½" x 20")

1. Referring to "Constructing Units from Paired Fabrics" on page 18, pair each of the yellow 5½" x 20" strips with a blue 5½" x 20" strip. Cut two sets of paired fabrics into two 5½" squares. Cut the 5½" squares once diagonally. Cut the remaining two sets of paired fabrics into four 2½" x 5½" segments. Set the end pieces aside to use later.

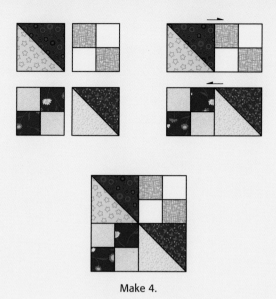

Make 4.

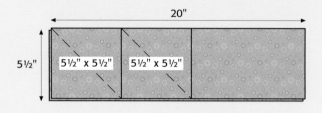

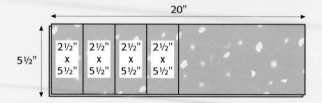

2. Referring to "Half-Square-Triangle Units" on page 19, make eight half-square-triangle units. Trim to 4½".

3. Referring to "Four-Patch Units" on page 19, make eight four-patch units.

4. Arrange the units made in steps 2 and 3 into four identical blocks as shown. *Make certain the units within each block are positioned correctly.* Sew the pieces of each block together in rows and press the seams toward the four-patch units. Sew the rows together and press the seams open.

5. Repeat steps 1–4 until you've completed 28 blocks.

6. Arrange the 28 blocks on a design wall. Decide which fabrics you find most pleasing. In the first step, 28 paired fabrics were set aside. From these, choose eight to be used for half-square-triangle units and eight to be used for four-patch units. If a fabric was used for four-patch units before, consider using it for half-square triangles this time. Cut the paired fabrics as shown. From the eight for half-square triangles, cut one 5½" square. From the eight for four-patch units, cut two 2½" x 5½" pieces.

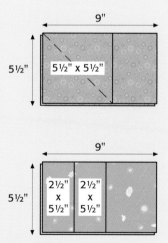

7. Make 16 half-square-triangle units and 16 four-patch units. Carefully arrange the units into eight blocks and sew the blocks together as you did before.

## Assembling the Quilt Top

1. On a design wall, arrange the blocks into seven horizontal rows of five blocks each. You'll have one extra block. Scatter the blocks that use the same fabrics. Referring to the quilt diagram, turn the blocks until diagonal lines are formed. If this seems impossible, one or more of the blocks may be incorrectly pieced. For the design to work, the four-patch units and half-square-triangle units of each block must be in the correct positions.

Quilt diagram

2. Sew the blocks into horizontal rows. Press the seams open.

3. Join the rows. Press the seams open.

4. If the light blue inner borders were cut from a stripe on the lengthwise grain, refer to "Adding Borders" on page 25. If the light blue inner borders were cut across the grain of the fabric, refer to "Joining Border Strips" on page 25. Cut two of the 2"-wide light blue strips into two equal lengths. Using a diagonal seam, sew a half strip to the end of each full-length strip. Press the seams open. Add the inner borders.

5. Add the medium blue outer borders, using the 6½" x 64" strips.

## Finishing the Quilt

1. Cut the backing fabric, across the grain, into two equal pieces. Remove the selvages. Sew these pieces together along the lengthwise grain to create the quilt back. Press the seam open. The seam will run horizontally across the quilt.

2. Refer to "Layering and Basting" on page 26.

3. Hand or machine quilt as desired.

4. Refer to "Binding" on page 27 and use the medium blue 2½"-wide strips to bind the quilt.

5. Make and attach a label to your quilt.

# Texas Two-Step: Wild West Shuffle

Made by Lynn Roddy Brown with help from Nancy Brown, Karen King, Nancy Milrany, Betsey Sevy,
Janice Thompson, and the Ladies from Nederland. Block designed by Jackie Theriot.

This quilt is totally scrappy, with an overall pattern created by light and dark values. I selected fabrics from what I call my ugly stash—fabrics with unusual textures and multiple colors. Four of my friends agreed to help sew blocks. I provided each of them with sets of fabric strips to make four blocks. They received a lesson in making scrap quilts and I got to keep the blocks. I did this a second time with a lovely group of ladies from Nederland, Texas. My students were not delighted with my fabric choices because they felt they didn't match. After the blocks were made and on the design wall, they began to see that scrap blocks based solely on value could work to make a wonderful quilt.

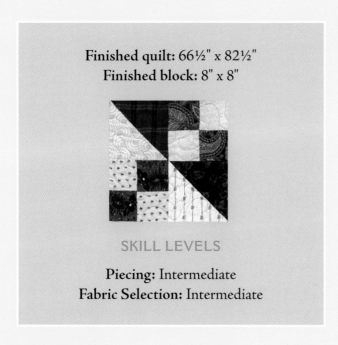

Finished quilt: 66½" x 82½"
Finished block: 8" x 8"

SKILL LEVELS

Piecing: Intermediate
Fabric Selection: Intermediate

## Materials

*All yardages are based on 42"-wide fabric unless otherwise noted.*

+ 2¼ yards of navy blue print for outer border
+ 1⅓ yards of gold print for inner border and binding
+ 36 scrap strips, 5½" x 20", of different medium to dark prints for blocks
+ 36 scrap strips, 5½" x 20", of different light prints for blocks
+ 5½ yards of fabric for backing
+ 75" x 91" piece of batting

## Cutting

**From the gold print, cut:**
+ 15 strips, 2½" x 42"

**From the navy blue print, cut:**
+ 4 strips, 7½" x 72", from the lengthwise grain

## Making the Blocks

Blocks are made in sets of four. For each set of blocks, you'll need:
+ 4 scrap strips of medium to dark prints (5½" x 20")
+ 4 scrap strips of light prints (5½" x 20")

1.  Referring to "Constructing Units from Paired Fabrics" on page 18, pair each of the medium to dark strips with a light strip. Cut each of the four sets of paired fabrics into one 5½" square and two 2½" x 5½" segments as shown. Cut the 5½" squares once diagonally. Set aside the end pieces to use later.

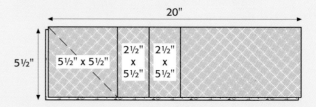

2.  Refer to "Half-Square-Triangle Units" on page 19 to make eight half-square-triangle units. Trim to 4½".

3. Referring to "Four-Patch Units" on page 19, make eight four-patch units.

4. Using the eight half-square-triangle units and eight four-patch units made in steps 2 and 3, arrange the pieces into four blocks as shown. Each block should have two different four-patch units and two different half-square-triangle units. All eight of the fabrics selected for the set will be in each block. *Make certain the units within each block are positioned correctly.*

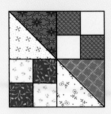 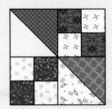

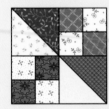 

5. Sew the pieces of each block together in rows and press the seams toward the four-patch unit. Sew the rows together and press the seams open.

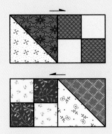 

6. Repeat steps 1–5 until you've completed 36 blocks.

7. Arrange the 36 blocks on a design wall. Decide which fabrics you find most pleasing. In the first step, 36 pieces of paired fabrics were set aside. From these, choose 12 paired fabrics to be used for half-square-triangle units. Cut one

5½" square from each; cut the squares once diagonally. Choose 12 of the paired fabrics to be used for four-patch units and cut two 2½"-wide segments from each as shown.

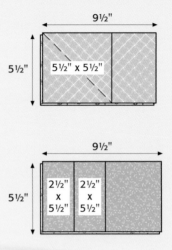

8. Make 24 half-square-triangle units and 24 four-patch units. Carefully arrange the units into 12 blocks. Refer to step 5 to complete the blocks.

## Assembling the Quilt Top

1. On a design wall, arrange the blocks into eight horizontal rows of six blocks each. Scatter the blocks, using the same fabrics, and turn groups of four blocks until they form a 16-patch unit. If this seems impossible, one or more of the blocks may be incorrectly pieced. For the design to work, the four-patch units and half-square-triangle units of each block must be in the correct positions.

2. Sew the horizontal rows. Press the seams open.

3. Join the rows. Press the seams open.

4. Refer to "Joining Border Strips" on page 25. For each of the gold side inner borders, use two 2½"-wide strips. Sew these strips end to end, using a diagonal seam. Press the seams open. To make the top and bottom inner borders, cut one of the 2½"-wide gold strips into two equal lengths. Using a diagonal seam, sew these half strips to gold full-length strips. Press the seams open.

5. Refer to "Adding Borders" on page 25 to add the gold inner borders.

6. Add the navy outer borders, using the 7½" x 72" strips.

## Finishing the Quilt

1. Cut the backing fabric, across the grain, into two equal pieces. Remove the selvages. Sew these pieces together along the lengthwise grain to create the quilt back. Press the seam open. The seam will run vertically on the quilt.

2. Refer to "Layering and Basting" on page 26.

3. Hand or machine quilt as desired.

4. Refer to "Binding" on page 27 and use the remaining gold 2½"-wide strips to bind the quilt.

5. Make and attach a label to your quilt.

## Color Option

Carrousel, made by Lynn Roddy Brown.
Block design by Jackie Theriot.
Finished quilt: 56½" x 72½"
Finished block: 8" x 8"

This quilt is made using the same block as in "Wild West Shuffle" (page 64), but it uses related fabrics with a common background fabric rather than a completely scrappy approach. The uneven set (five by seven blocks) gives "Carrousel" more energy than "Wild West Shuffle."

# Bow Ties: Amish Bow Ties

Made by Lynn Roddy Brown with help from her daughter Nancy. Hand quilting in blocks by Mary Tomlinson.

In her book *An Amish Adventure*, Roberta Horton states that the Pennsylvania Amish eliminated orange, yellow, and yellow-green from their color palette, and black was the only neutral used. I've made several Amish-style quilts and have found this to be a no-fail formula.

To make this quilt, I selected 26 solid fabrics from my stash and made 52 blocks. My original plan was to set the blocks on point, but the quilt looked disjointed and spotty. I tried using a straight set with the Bow Ties forming diagonal lines. I was still not completely satisfied, so I sorted the blocks by color. When I could not make a diagonal line all one color, I used a similar color and value. In the end, I used 48 of the blocks and was happy with the results.

Remember, your first plan may not work. Just because you've made a block doesn't mean you have to use it.

**Finished quilt: 53½" x 65½"**
**Finished block: 6" x 6"**

SKILL LEVELS

**Piecing:** Easy
**Fabric Selection:** Easy

## Materials

*All yardages are based on 42"-wide fabric unless otherwise noted.*

- 2⅝ yards of black solid for block backgrounds and outer border
- ⅝ yard of dark pink solid for inner border
- 24 scrap strips, 5½" x 20", of different solid colors for blocks

- ¾ yard of dark green solid for binding*
- 3¾ yards of fabric for backing
- 62" x 74" piece of batting

*\*I used ½"-wide binding for this quilt; wide bindings are typical of Amish quilts. If you use a narrower binding, ⅝ yard will be enough.*

## Cutting

**From the black solid, cut:**
- 4 strips, 7" x 58", from the lengthwise grain
- 2 strips, 3½" x 58", from the lengthwise grain; crosscut into 30 squares, 3½" x 3½"
- 6 strips, 3½" x 42"; crosscut into 66 squares, 3½" x 3½"

**From the dark pink solid, cut:**
- 6 strips, 2½" x 42"

**From the dark green solid, cut:**
- 7 strips, 3¼" x 42"*

*\*Cut 2½"-wide strips if you want a narrower binding.*

## Making the Blocks

Blocks are made in sets of two. For each set of blocks, you'll need:
- 1 scrap strip of solid color (5½" x 20")
- 4 black 3½" squares

1. Cut the scrap strip into four 2" squares and four 3½" squares as shown.

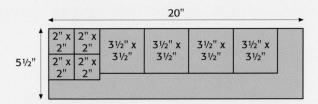

2. Refer to "Folded-Corner Triangles" on page 20. Sew a colored 2" square from step 1 on the corner of each black 3½" square to make four bow-tie units.

Make 4.

3. Lay out two bow-tie units from step 2 and two colored 3½" squares as shown. Sew the pieces together in rows and press the seams toward the colored squares. Sew the rows together and press the seam open. Repeat to make the second block.

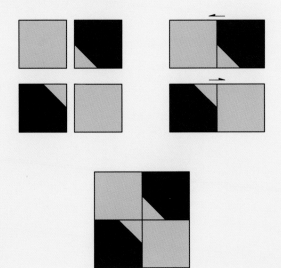

4. Repeat steps 1–3 until you've made 48 blocks.

## Assembling the Quilt Top

1. Following the quilt diagram, arrange the blocks in eight horizontal rows of six blocks each. Turn the Bow Tie blocks to form diagonal lines. Consider sorting the blocks by color or value. Your decision depends on your particular group of blocks and the arrangement that you find most pleasing.

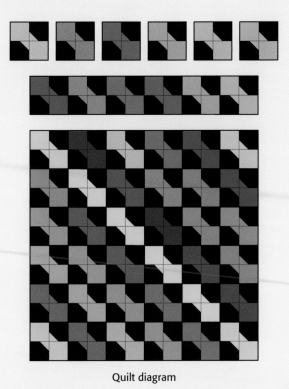

Quilt diagram

2. Sew the horizontal rows together. Press the seams open.

3. Join the rows. Press the seams open.

4. Refer to "Joining Border Strips" on page 25. Cut two of the 2½"-wide pink strips into two equal lengths. Using a diagonal seam, sew each of these half strips to the end of a full-length strip.

5. Refer to "Adding Borders" on page 25. Add the pink inner borders.

6.  Add the black outer borders, using the 7" x 58" strips.

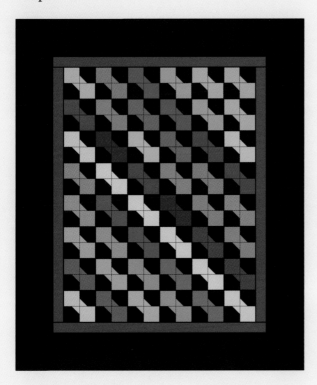

## Finishing the Quilt

1.  Cut the backing fabric, across the grain, into two equal pieces. Remove the selvages. Sew these pieces together along the lengthwise grain to create the quilt back. Press the seam open. The seam will run horizontally across the quilt.

2.  Refer to "Layering and Basting" on page 26.

3.  Hand or machine quilt as desired.

4.  Refer to "Binding" on page 27 and use the green 3¼"-wide strips to bind the quilt. Sew, using a ½" seam allowance, and stop ½" from each corner.

5.  Make and attach a label to your quilt.

# Bow Ties: Bow Tie Circles

Made by Lynn Roddy Brown with help from her daughter Nancy

For this quilt, I chose fabrics with a lot of different visual textures. I sorted the fabrics in two piles—light and medium to dark. I didn't use fabrics that seemed to fall between the two piles. This difference in values defined the pattern. Borders made from the same-size blocks as those used in the body of the quilt fit perfectly when the inner borders continue through the outer borders.

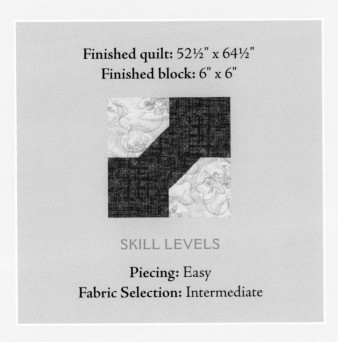

Finished quilt: 52½" x 64½"
Finished block: 6" x 6"

SKILL LEVELS

**Piecing:** Easy
**Fabric Selection:** Intermediate

## Materials

*All yardages are based on 42"-wide fabric unless otherwise noted.*

+ ⅝ yard of purple print for inner borders
+ 40 scrap strips, 5½" x 20", of different medium to dark prints for blocks
+ 40 scrap strips, 5½" x 20", of different light prints for blocks
+ ⅝ yard of purple stripe for binding*
+ 3⅔ yards of fabric for backing
+ 61" x 73" piece of batting

*For bias binding, you'll need 1 yard to make a total length of 246".*

## Cutting

**From the purple print, cut:**
+ 7 strips, 2½" x 42"

**From the purple stripe, cut:**
+ 7 strips, 2½" x 42", for straight-grain binding

## Making the Blocks

Blocks are made in sets of two. For each set of blocks, you'll need:

+ 1 scrap strip of medium to dark print (5½" x 20")
+ 1 scrap strip of light print (5½" x 20")

1. Cut the medium to dark strip into four 2" squares and four 3½" squares as shown. From the light strip, cut four 3½" squares.

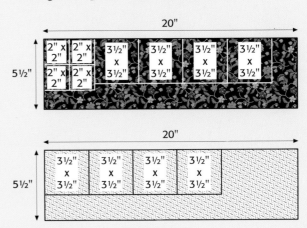

2. Referring to "Folded-Corner Triangles" on page 20, sew a medium to dark 2" square on the corner of each light 3½" square to make four bow-tie units.

Make 4.

3. Lay out two bow-tie units from step 2 and two medium to dark 3½" squares as shown. Sew the pieces together in rows and press the seams toward the medium to dark squares. Sew the rows together and press the seams open. Repeat to make the second block.

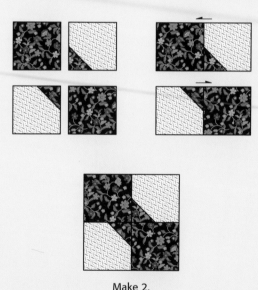

Make 2.

4. Repeat steps 1–3 until you've made 80 blocks.

## Assembling the Quilt Top

1. The blocks were made in pairs. I separated them into two groups with the identical blocks in different stacks. I started with one stack and arranged the blocks in horizontal rows of six blocks each, alternating the direction of the bow tie from block to block to create the "circles." When I had used the entire first stack, I picked up the second stack and used enough blocks to complete the body of the quilt (eight horizontal rows of six blocks each). I used the remainder of the second stack for the borders. Refer to the quilt diagram on page 75 to make certain all the blocks are in the correct position.

2. Sew the blocks into horizontal rows. Press the seams open.

3. Sew the rows together. Press the seams open.

4. Sew the six blocks of the top border together. Press the seams open. Use six more blocks to piece the bottom border.

5. Measure across the center of the quilt body, and trim the purple strips to this length for the top and bottom inner borders. Sew one strip to each of the border sections. Attach the top and bottom borders.

6. Cut one purple strip into four 2½" x 6½" strips. Following the quilt diagram, piece each side border, using 10 Bow Tie blocks and two purple strips.

7. Using a diagonal seam, sew two 2½" x 42" purple strips end to end for each side inner border. Measure lengthwise through the center of the quilt. Trim the inner borders to this measurement.

8. Sew the purple inner side borders to the pieced side borders.

9. Attach the side borders, making sure the horizontal inner borders are aligned.

Quilt diagram

## Finishing the Quilt

1. Cut the backing fabric, across the grain, into two equal pieces. Remove the selvages. Sew these pieces together along the lengthwise grain to create the quilt back. Press the seam open. The seam will run horizontally across the quilt.

2. Refer to "Layering and Basting" on page 26.

3. Hand or machine quilt as desired.

4. Refer to "Binding" on page 27 and use the 2½"-wide stripe strips to bind the quilt.

5. Make and attach a label to your quilt.

# Spools: Scrappy Spools

Made by Lynn Roddy Brown with traded blocks

This quilt is the result of a block trade. Because the blocks stand alone, fabrics with many different textures and values can be used successfully. A medium pink stripe, cut on the bias so the stripes fall at an angle, keeps the binding from blending in with the blocks.

Most of the blocks in this quilt have light backgrounds with medium to dark spools. But if you look closely, you'll see some blocks that almost fade into the background because they are made using similar values—a trick I learned from author Darra Williamson for adding impact to the quilt.

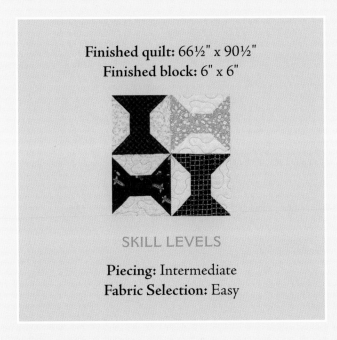

Finished quilt: 66½" x 90½"
Finished block: 6" x 6"

SKILL LEVELS

Piecing: Intermediate
Fabric Selection: Easy

## Materials

*All yardages are based on 42"-wide fabric unless otherwise noted.*

+ 84 scrap strips, 5½" x 20", of different medium to dark prints for blocks
+ 56 scrap strips, 5½" x 20", of different light prints for blocks
+ ¾ yard of pink stripe for straight-grain binding*
+ 6 yards of fabric for backing
+ 75" x 99" piece of batting

*For bias binding, you'll need 1¼ yards for a total length of 326".*

## Cutting

**From the pink stripe, cut:**
+ 9 strips, 2½" x 42" (straight-grain binding)

## Making the Blocks

Blocks are made in sets of six. For each set of blocks, you'll need:
+ 3 scrap strips of medium to dark prints (5½" x 20")
+ 2 scrap strips of light prints (5½" x 20")

1. Cut each of the three medium to dark strips into two rectangles, 2½" x 6½", and eight 2½" squares as shown.

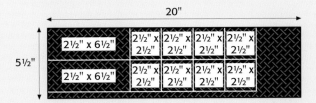

2. Cut each of the two light strips into six rectangles, 2½" x 6½" as shown.

3. Refer to "Folded-Corner Triangles" on page 20. Using four matching 2½" squares and two matching 2½" x 6½" light strips, sew the squares to opposite corners of the rectangles to make two spool units. Repeat until you have six pairs of spool units.

Make 6 pairs.

4. Place pairs of spool units on each side of a matching medium or dark 2½" x 6½" rectangle as shown. Sew the two seams. Press toward the middle. Repeat to make the six blocks.

Make 2 of each medium/dark print.

5. Repeat steps 1–4 until you've completed 168 blocks.

## Assembling the Quilt Top

1. Referring to the quilt diagram at right, arrange the blocks on a design wall in 15 horizontal rows of 11 blocks each. Alternate the horizontal and vertical placement of the blocks. Be sure to scatter the blocks that are made with the same fabric set across the surface of the quilt. You'll have three extra blocks.

2. Join the blocks to form rows. Press the seams open.

3. Join the rows. Press the seams open.

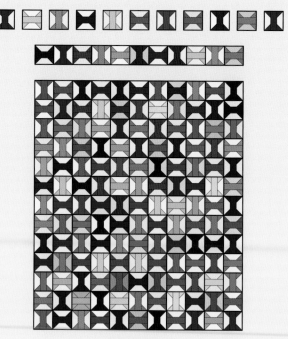

Quilt diagram

## Finishing the Quilt

1. Cut the backing fabric, across the grain, into two equal pieces. Remove the selvages. Sew these pieces together along the lengthwise grain to create the back. Press this seam open. The seam will run vertically on the quilt.

2. Refer to "Layering and Basting" on page 26.

3. Hand or machine quilt as desired.

4. Refer to "Binding" on page 27 and use the stripe 2½"-wide strips to bind the quilt.

5. Make and attach a label to your quilt.

# Spools: Floating Spools

Made by Lynn Roddy Brown with help from her daughter Nancy

For this quilt, I chose bright children's prints that contrast well with the black dot background. Two blocks made from a dark blue print were eliminated because they seemed to disappear into the background.

I wanted to set these Spool blocks on point, but when I arranged them on the design wall with the setting triangles, it created a very oddly shaped edge. I added a black inner border that made the blocks "float" and this solved the problem.

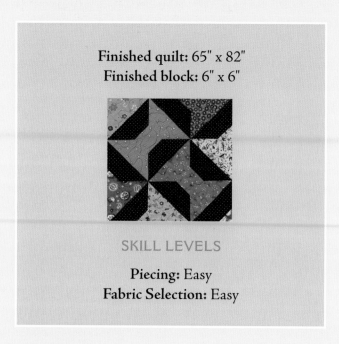

Finished quilt: 65" x 82"
Finished block: 6" x 6"

SKILL LEVELS

Piecing: Easy
Fabric Selection: Easy

## Materials

*All yardages are based on 42"-wide fabric unless otherwise noted.*

+ 5¼ yards of black dot fabric for blocks, inner and outer borders, and setting triangles
+ ½ yard of teal print for middle border
+ 30 scrap strips, 5½" x 20", of different bright prints for blocks
+ ¾ yard of hot pink print for binding
+ 5½ yards of fabric for backing
+ 73" x 90" piece of batting

## Cutting

**From the black dot fabric, cut:**
+ 20 strips, 2½" x 42"; crosscut into 120 rectangles, 2½" x 6½"
+ 3 strips, 3" x 42"
+ 2 strips, 11" x 42"; crosscut into 5 squares, 11" x 11". Cut each square twice diagonally to yield 20 side triangles.
+ 2 squares, 6½" x 6½". Cut each square once diagonally to yield 4 corner triangles.
+ 2 strips, 3" x 72", from the lengthwise grain
+ 4 strips, 7½" x 72", from the lengthwise grain

**From the teal print, cut:**
+ 7 strips, 2" x 42"

**From the hot pink print, cut:**
+ 8 strips, 2½" x 42"

## Making the Blocks

Blocks are made in sets of two. For each set of blocks, you'll need:
+ 1 scrap strip of bright print (5½" x 20")
+ 4 rectangles of black dot fabric, 2½" x 6½"

1. Cut the bright strip into two rectangles, 2½" x 6½", and eight 2½" squares as shown.

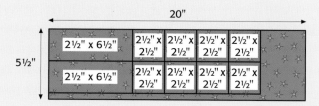

2.  Refer to "Folded-Corner Triangles" on page 20. Using the eight bright 2½" squares and four 2½" x 6½" black rectangles, sew the squares to opposite corners of the rectangles to make four spool units.

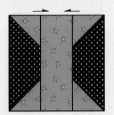

Make 4.

3.  Place pairs of spool units on each side of a bright rectangle as shown. Sew the two seams. Press toward the bright rectangle. Make the second block.

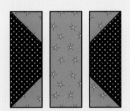

Make 2.

4.  Repeat steps 1–3 until you've completed 60 blocks.

## Assembling the Quilt Top

1.  Referring to the quilt diagram at right, arrange the blocks, setting triangles, and corner triangles in a diagonal set on a design wall. As you arrange the blocks, be sure to separate the identical ones and alternate the orientation of the spools. You'll have one extra block.

Quilt diagram

2.  Referring to "Diagonal Sets" on page 24, sew the side-setting triangles and blocks together into diagonal rows. Press the seams open.

3.  Join the rows. Press the seams open. Add the corner triangles.

4.  Referring to "Diagonal Sets," trim the quilt so that you have a ¼" inch seam allowance on the outside edges.

5.  Refer to "Adding Borders" on page 25. Add the black 3" x 72" inner borders to the sides of the quilt. Refer to "Joining Border Strips" on page 25. To make the top and bottom inner borders, cut one of the black 3" x 42" strips into two equal lengths. Using a straight seam, sew one half strip to the end of each full-length strip. Press the seam open. Add the top and bottom inner borders.

6. For each of the teal side middle borders, use two 2"-wide strips. Sew these strips end to end, using a diagonal seam. Press the seams open. To make the top and bottom middle borders, cut one of the 2"-wide teal strips into two equal lengths. Using a diagonal seam, sew a half strip to the end of each full-length strip. Press the seams open. Add the teal middle borders.

7. Add the black outer borders, using the 7½" x 72" strips.

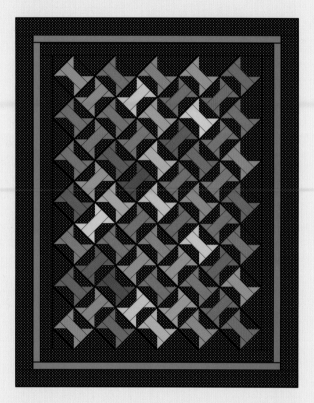

## Finishing the Quilt

1. Cut the backing fabric, across the grain, into two equal pieces. Remove the selvages. Sew these pieces together along the lengthwise grain to create the quilt back. Press the seam open. The seam will run vertically on the quilt.

2. Refer to "Layering and Basting" on page 26.

3. Hand or machine quilt as desired.

4. Refer to "Binding" on page 27 and use the pink 2½"-wide strips to bind the quilt.

5. Make and attach a label to your quilt.

# Hourglass: Nana's Pinwheels

Made by Lynn Roddy Brown with help from her daughter Nancy

Each of the large blocks in Nana's Pinwheels uses 16 different 1930s-reproduction fabrics. Units for the large blocks are made from four fabrics in different colors. A few of the fabrics in my collection are much darker in value than others. When I selected each set of four fabrics, I did not use more than one dark. This helped scatter the dark fabrics over the surface.

The medium blue used in the sashing and outer border has less visual texture than the fabrics used in the blocks. This helps separate the blocks and lets them stand out. Using red, which is always a strong color, allows the cornerstones to show and provides a sharp frame around the quilt when used for the inner border and binding.

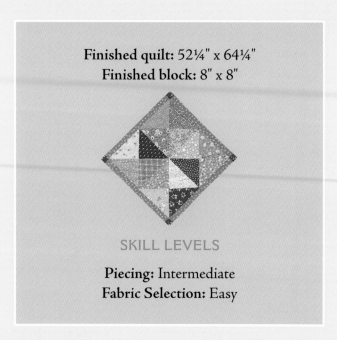

Finished quilt: 52¼" x 64¼"
Finished block: 8" x 8"

SKILL LEVELS

Piecing: Intermediate
Fabric Selection: Easy

## Materials

*All yardages are based on 42"-wide fabric unless otherwise noted.*

+ 2¼ yards of medium blue print for sashing and outer border
+ 1 yard of light blue print for setting triangles
+ ⅞ yard of red print for sashing squares, inner border, and binding
+ 24 scrap strips, 5½" x 20", of different 1930s-reproduction fabrics for blocks
+ 3⅔ yards of fabric for backing
+ 60" x 72" piece of batting

## Cutting

**From the medium blue print, cut:**
+ 4 strips, 7½" x 60", from the lengthwise grain
+ 12 strips, 1" x 42"; crosscut into 48 strips, 1" x 8½"*

**From the red print, cut:**
+ 6 strips, 1" x 42"; crosscut 1 strip into 32 squares, 1" x 1"
+ 7 strips, 2½" x 42"

**From the light blue print, cut:**
+ 2 strips, 14½" x 42"; crosscut into 3 squares, 14½" x 14½". Cut each square twice diagonally to yield 12 side triangles (2 are extra).
+ 2 squares, 8½" x 8½". Cut each square once diagonally to yield 4 corner triangles.

*\*Wait until the blocks are completed to cut the sashing strips.*

## Making the Quarter-Square-Triangle Units

Units are made in sets of 12. Make all the units before sewing the blocks together. For each set, you'll need:

+ 4 scrap strips of 1930s-reproduction prints in different colors (5½" x 20")

1. Referring to "Constructing Units from Paired Fabrics" on page 18, create two sets of paired fabrics, using the 5½" x 20" strips. Cut each set into three 5½" squares. Cut the squares once diagonally as shown.

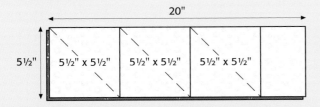

2. Sew the diagonal seams of the triangle pairs made in step 1. Press the seams to one side. You should have 12 half-square-triangle units. Sort the units into two groups with six identical units in each group.

Make 6.            Make 6.

3. Place a half-square-triangle unit from each group on a cutting mat with right sides together, aligning the edges and nesting the opposing seams. Cut the nested pair diagonally across the seam. Before moving the units from the mat, place one pin in each unit to hold the nested seam. Sew the seam and press open. Repeat until you have 12 quarter-square-triangle units.

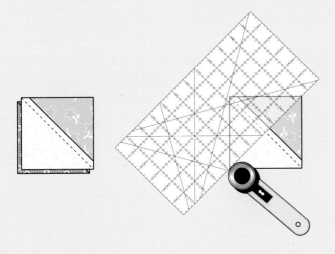

4. Trim the quarter-square-triangle units to 4½" square by placing the 45° diagonal line of a small square ruler along one of the seam lines. Position the 2¼" mark of the ruler on the unit center. Trim the two adjacent sides. Reposition the unit so the trimmed edges are under the ruler on the 4½" mark. Trim the remaining sides. Repeat for all 12 units.

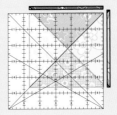 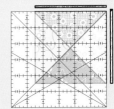

Trim units 4½" square.

5. Repeat steps 1–4 until you've completed 72 units.

## Making the Blocks

1. Sort the 72 completed units into six groups of 12 units each; the units in each group will be made of the same fabrics.

Make 12.       Make 12.       Make 12.

Make 12.       Make 12.       Make 12.

2. Select four different units at random for each block. Arrange the four units into rows as shown. Turn the units until you find them pleasing. I tried to avoid having the same colors touching. Sew the units together in rows and press the seams open. Sew the rows together and press the seams open. Repeat until you've completed 18 blocks.

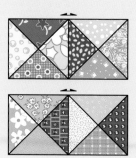 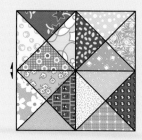

Make 18.

Quilt diagram

3. The blocks should measure 8½" square. Mine were consistently 8⅜" square, so I used that measurement to cut the 48 sashing strips. Use your block measurement to cut the 48 sashing strips.

## Assembling the Quilt Top

1. Referring to the quilt diagram at right, arrange the blocks on your design wall in a diagonal set. Move or turn the blocks until you're happy with the arrangement. Add the sashing strips, sashing squares, and setting triangles.

2. Refer to "Diagonal Sets" on page 24 to join the blocks and sashing into diagonal rows. Press the seams toward the sashing.

3. Sew the remaining sashing and sashing squares into rows. Press toward the sashing. Join the sashing rows and block rows as shown, and then add the side-setting triangles. Press toward the sashing. Sew the rows together and add the corner-setting triangles last. Referring to "Diagonal Sets," trim the quilt on all four sides, leaving a ¼" seam allowance.

4. Refer to "Adding Borders" on page 25. Add the top and bottom red borders first, using one 1"-wide strip for each. Refer to "Joining Border Strips" on page 25. Cut one of the 1"-wide red strips into two equal lengths. Using a diagonal seam, sew a half strip to the end of each full-length strip. Press the seam open. Add the side inner borders.

5. Add the side outer borders first and then the top and bottom, using the medium blue 7½" x 60" strips.

## Finishing the Quilt

1. Cut the backing fabric, across the grain, into two equal pieces. Remove the selvages. Sew these pieces together along the lengthwise grain to create the back. Press the seam open. The seam will run horizontally across the quilt.

2. Refer to "Layering and Basting" on page 26.

3. Hand or machine quilt as desired.

4. Refer to "Binding" on page 27 and use the red 2½"-wide strips to bind the quilt.

5. Make and attach a label to your quilt.

# Hourglass: Thank You, Marsha

Made by Lynn Roddy Brown

Marsha McCloskey has made many wonderful quilts using Ohio Stars and large-scale floral fabrics. With this quilt, I was inspired by her book *On to Square Two*.

When selecting the fabrics, first choose six pink fabrics and six brown fabrics for the star points. Then choose a background fabric for the blocks that will provide high contrast with the star points. Once your blocks are complete, have fun choosing the fabric for the setting blocks and the floral print for the borders and setting triangles.

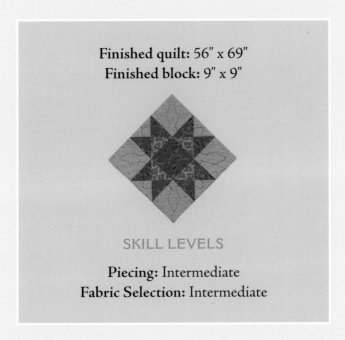

Finished quilt: 56" x 69"
Finished block: 9" x 9"

SKILL LEVELS

Piecing: Intermediate
Fabric Selection: Intermediate

## Materials

*All yardages are based on 42"-wide fabric unless otherwise noted.*

+ 3 yards of large-scale floral print for setting triangles and outer border
+ ⅞ yard of light tan print for block backgrounds
+ ⅔ yard of medium pink print 1 for setting blocks
+ ⅓ yard of medium pink print 2 for inner border
+ 6 scrap strips, 5½" x 20", of different pink prints for blocks
+ 6 scrap strips, 5½" x 20", of different brown prints for blocks
+ ⅔ yard of dark pink print for binding
+ 4 yards of fabric for backing
+ 64" x 77" piece of batting

## Cutting

**From the light tan print, cut:**
+ 5 strips, 3½" x 42"; crosscut into 48 squares, 3½" x 3½"
+ 2 strips, 4½" x 42"; crosscut into 12 squares, 4½" x 4½"

**From the large-scale floral print, cut:**
+ 2 strips, 15" x 42"; crosscut into 3 squares, 15" x 15". Cut each square twice diagonally to yield 12 side triangles (2 are extra).
+ 2 squares, 8½" x 8½"; cut each square once diagonally to yield 4 corner triangles
+ 4 strips, 8¼" x 60", cut from the lengthwise grain

**From medium pink print 1, cut:**
+ 6 squares, 9½" x 9½"*

**From medium pink print 2, cut:**
+ 5 strips, 1½" x 42"

**From the dark pink print, cut:**
+ 7 strips, 2½" x 42"

*Wait until the Star blocks are completed to cut the setting squares.*

## Making the Blocks

Blocks are made in sets of two. For each set of blocks, you'll need:

✦ 1 pink scrap strip (5½" x 20")
✦ 1 brown scrap strip (5½" x 20")
✦ 8 tan 3½" squares
✦ 2 tan 4½" squares

1. Cut both the pink strip and the brown strip into three 4½" squares and one 3½" square as shown.

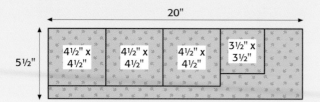

2. Refer to "Constructing Units from Paired Fabrics" on page 18. Pair a pink 4½" square with a brown 4½" square, and a pink 4½" square with a tan 4½" square. Cut each of the paired fabrics diagonally to form two triangles. Sew the diagonal seams and press toward the pink to make two A half-square-triangle units and two B half-square-triangle units.

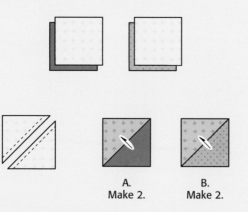

A.
Make 2.

B.
Make 2.

3. To make pink star-point units, select an A unit and a B unit from step 2. Place right sides together, aligning the edges and nesting the opposing seams. Check to make certain the pink side of the units is on opposite sides of the nested seam. Cut diagonally across the seam lines. Sew the seams and press open. Make four.

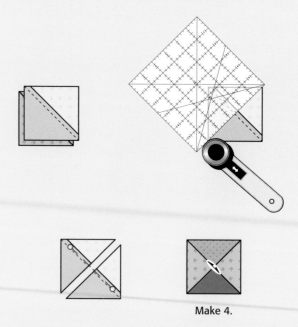

Make 4.

4. Pair a brown 4½" square with a pink 4½" square, and a brown 4½" square with a tan 4½" square. Cut each of the paired fabrics diagonally to form two triangles. Sew the diagonal seams and press toward the brown to make two X half-square-triangle units and two Y half-square-triangle units.

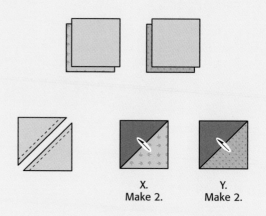

X.
Make 2.

Y.
Make 2.

5. To make brown star-point units, select an X unit and a Y unit from step 4. Place right sides together, aligning the edges and nesting the opposing seams. Check to make certain the brown of the units is on opposite sides of the nested seam. Cut diagonally across the seam lines. Sew the seams and press open. Make four.

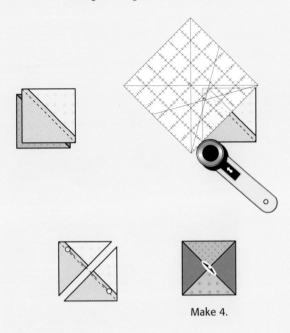

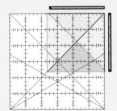

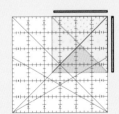

Make 4.

6. Trim each star-point unit to 3½" square by placing the 45° diagonal line of a small square ruler along one of the seam lines. Position the 1¾" mark of the ruler on the center of the star-point unit. Trim the two adjacent sides. Rotate the unit so the trimmed edges are under the ruler on the 3½" mark. Trim the remaining sides.

Trim units 3½" square.

7. Lay out the star-point units, the eight 3½" tan squares, the 3½" pink square, and the 3½" brown square into two Star blocks as shown. Sew the pieces together in rows, pressing the seams toward the squares. Join the rows. Press the seams open. Repeat until you've made 12 blocks.

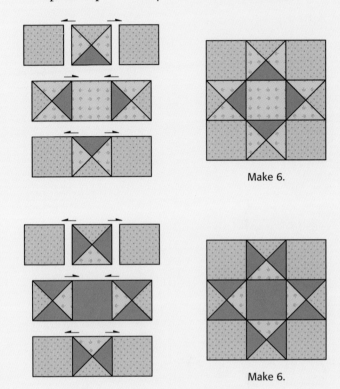

Make 6.

Make 6.

## Assembling the Quilt Top

1.  The Star blocks should be 9½" square. This is the measurement to use for cutting the setting blocks. If your blocks are slightly smaller or larger, use your measurement. Cut six squares from medium pink print 1 for the setting blocks.

2.  Following the quilt diagram, arrange the Star blocks, the setting blocks, and the side-setting triangles into diagonal rows on a design wall. The Star blocks were made in pairs; be sure to separate them in the quilt.

Quilt diagram

3.  Referring to "Diagonal Sets" on page 24, join the Star blocks, setting blocks, and side-setting triangles into diagonal rows. Press away from the Star blocks.

4.  Join the rows. Press the seams open. Add the corner-setting triangles. Press outward. Referring to "Diagonal Sets," trim the quilt on all four sides, leaving a ¼" seam allowance.

5.  Refer to "Adding Borders" on page 25. Add the top and bottom medium pink inner borders, using one 1½"-wide strip for each. Refer to "Joining Border Strips" on page 25. To make the side inner borders, cut one of the 1½"-wide medium pink strips into two equal lengths. Using a diagonal seam, sew a half strip to the end of each full-length strip. Press the seam open. Add the side inner borders.

6.  Add the side outer borders and then the top and bottom, using the floral 8¼" x 60" strips.

## Finishing the Quilt

1.  Cut the backing fabric, across the grain, into two equal pieces. Remove the selvages. Sew these pieces together along the lengthwise grain to create the quilt back. Press the seam open. The seam will run horizontally across the quilt.

2.  Refer to "Layering and Basting" on page 26.

3.  Hand or machine quilt as desired.

4.  Refer to "Binding" on page 27 and use the dark pink 2½"-wide strips to bind the quilt.

5.  Make and attach a label to your quilt.

# About the Author

LYNN RODDY BROWN is a sixth-generation Texan who has always loved to sew. She took her first sewing lessons at the age of eight at the local Singer sewing-machine shop. When she was 10, she won the Singer regional dressmaking contest and received a sewing machine as her prize.

As she was growing up, there was one beautiful quilt in her home, made by Lynn's great-grandmother as a wedding gift for her parents. This quilt, which now belongs to Lynn, kindled a lifelong interest in quilting. In the early 1970s, she began tearing pictures of quilts from magazines and did some patchwork with templates, but it was not until 1989 when she lived in Rochester, New York, that she began to quilt seriously.

For the past nine years, she has been a member of a bee that trades blocks for scrap quilts. She loves scrap quilts because it gives her the opportunity to use many different fabrics. She has had three of her quilts hung in the IQA juried show in Houston, two of which were scrap quilts.

Lynn currently lives in Houston, Texas, with her husband, an economics professor at Rice University. She and her husband have also lived in Pennsylvania, New Jersey, and New York. They have three mostly grown children (Kim, Wes, and Nancy), one wonderful son-in-law (Craig), and one beautiful granddaughter (Lillian). Lynn has been a seventh-grade science teacher and computer programmer. She received a kidney transplant in January of 2002, for which she is truly grateful. Some of her other hobbies include genealogy and Western swing dancing with her husband.

# New and Bestselling Titles from

America's Best-Loved Craft & Hobby Books®
America's Best-Loved Knitting Books®

America's Best-Loved Quilt Books®

---

**NEW RELEASES**
Adoration Quilts
Better by the Dozen
Blessed Home Quilt, The
Hooked on Wool
It's a Wrap
Let's Quilt!
Origami Quilts
Over Easy
Primitive Gatherings
Quilt Revival
Sew One and You're Done
Scraps of Time
Simple Chenille Quilts
Simple Traditions
Simply Primitive
Surprisingly Simple Quilts
Two-Block Theme Quilts
Wheel of Mystery Quilts

**APPLIQUÉ**
Appliqué Takes Wing
Easy Appliqué Samplers
Garden Party
Raise the Roof
Stitch and Split Appliqué
Tea in the Garden

**LEARNING TO QUILT**
Happy Endings, Revised Edition
Loving Stitches, Revised Edition
Magic of Quiltmaking, The
Quilter's Quick Reference Guide, The
Your First Quilt Book (or it should be!)

**PAPER PIECING**
40 Bright and Bold Paper-Pieced Blocks
50 Fabulous Paper-Pieced Stars
300 Paper-Pieced Quilt Blocks
Easy Machine Paper Piecing
Quilt Block Bonanza
Quilter's Ark, A
Show Me How to Paper Piece

**PIECING**
40 Fabulous Quick-Cut Quilts
101 Fabulous Rotary-Cut Quilts
365 Quilt Blocks a Year: Perpetual
  Calendar
1000 Great Quilt Blocks
Big 'n Easy
Clever Quilts Encore
Once More around the Block
Stack a New Deck

**QUILTS FOR BABIES & CHILDREN**
American Doll Quilts
Even More Quilts for Baby
More Quilts for Baby
Quilts for Baby
Sweet and Simple Baby Quilts

**SCRAP QUILTS**
More Nickel Quilts
Nickel Quilts
Save the Scraps
Successful Scrap Quilts
  from Simple Rectangles
Treasury of Scrap Quilts, A

**TOPICS IN QUILTMAKING**
Alphabet Soup
Cottage-Style Quilts
Creating Your Perfect Quilting Space
Focus on Florals
Follow the Dots . . . to Dazzling Quilts
More Biblical Quilt Blocks
Scatter Garden Quilts
Sensational Sashiko
Warm Up to Wool

**CRAFTS**
Bag Boutique
Purely Primitive
Scrapbooking Off the Page…and on the
  Wall
Stamp in Color
Vintage Workshop, The: Gifts for All
  Occasions

**KNITTING & CROCHET**
200 Knitted Blocks
365 Knitting Stitches a Year: Perpetual
  Calendar
Crochet from the Heart
First Crochet
First Knits
Fun and Funky Crochet
Handknit Style
Knits from the Heart
Little Box of Knitted Ponchos and Wraps,
  The
Little Box of Knitted Throws, The
Little Box of Crocheted Hats and Scarves,
  The
Little Box of Scarves, The
Little Box of Scarves II, The
Little Box of Sweaters, The
Pursenalities
Sensational Knitted Socks